# STEPS TO SELF LOVE AND CONFIDENCE

Kierre Shelton

# TABLE OF CONTENTS

# INTRODUCTION

❖ SELF LOVE AND CONFIDENCE

What is self-love?

Before a person can practice it, first, we need to understand what it means.

Self-love is a state of appreciation for oneself that grows from actions that support our physical, psychological, and spiritual growth. Self-love means having a high regard for your well-being and happiness. Self-love means taking care of your own needs and not sacrificing your well-being to please others. Self-love means not settling for less than you deserve.

Self-love can mean something different for each person because we all have many different ways to take care of ourselves. Figuring out what self-love looks like for you as an individual is an important part of your mental health.

For many people, the concept of self-love is an overblown theory, and they often ignore its importance. People aspire to be perfect, and perfectionism is considered a greater asset or attribute than self-love. When we talk about self-love, it is easy to picture someone reading self-help books or hugging a tree; but self-love is much more than that. Many studies have shown that self-love is the key to mental well-being, keeping depression and anxiety at bay.

Modern society is shaped to be bound to compete against each other constantly, or even ourselves. We are always trying to reach our short-term goals and trying to better ourselves to match the expectations set upon us by society. Many of us are guilty of working long hours and getting less sleep each night; we travel the extra mile and feel content to achieve perfectionism. We grind in and out every week; even during the weekend, 'relaxing' and 'having a good time' seem like a chore.

Consequently, we end up being too hard on ourselves all too often without even realizing it. All of us are more or less stuck up and consumed by our work, social interactions, life goals, weekend plans, and so on.

Love is the only thing that keeps us going and makes us less robotic in a world that requires us to work, think and act like programmed bots. Everyone needs love, and we spend most of our energy on loving others — be it friends, spouses, children, or family.

We all like to spread love, but the question is — do we produce enough for ourselves?

We cannot always expect to rely only on external sources for love, and that is where the concept of self-love comes in. A person who practices self-love will never need to depend on others to be happy, and it is an empowering feeling to be happy on the inside.

Self-love is not selfish; it is just putting yourself first and not being too tough on yourself. The next time you hear that little voice in your head telling you that you are not good enough or cannot afford to make mistakes, ignore it.

When our loved ones make a mistake, we often forgive them

easily, but we are often too hard on ourselves when we make a mistake.

The first step of self-love is realizing that we are only human and it is okay to make mistakes; it is okay to lose at times; it is okay not to have the best day...week...or month.

All we need to do is love ourselves and let the negative things pass through; eventually, things will change, and bad times will pass.

Self-love has many benefits; the first benefit is greater life satisfaction. When we love ourselves more, we instantly change our perspective of the world. Self-love can give us a more positive attitude towards life.

The second benefit of self-love is that it can encourage us to pick up good habits. Self-love means loving your body, soul, and mind. Therefore, people who love themselves often refrain from doing things that will impact their tranquility. Thus, it can help us adopt healthy habits.

If you start loving your body and mind more than others, you will not work during weekends; you will rather go on a drive or do some other activity that relaxes your mind.

Another important benefit of self-love is better mental health. People who love themselves are less likely to suffer from anxiety or depression; self-love also paves the way to a positive mindset, an essential ingredient for success in life and mental well-being.

Learning to love yourself also reduces stress, lessens procrastination, and makes you more focused at work.

Put yourself a little higher on your priority list; think highly of yourself as the world takes you at your estimate. If you have had a long day at work, come home and take a long break.

If you have had a tough week, take the weekend off and travel somewhere; get off your phone and give yourself some 'me time.' Consider yourself important, too; love yourself as much as you love your friends and family. Happiness and self-love are interconnected, and we all deserve to be happy. We must have our resolution on happiness; it recognizes happiness and well-being to be universal goals. Therefore, we should not strive to be perfect; rather, we should strive to love ourselves and pass on the love to others. Self-love is the key to happiness, and a person who is happy is in a far better position to achieve success in every aspect of life.

- Self Love is a Practice

Image result for self-love

Self-love is a practice, and it is something you learn and implement into your everyday life.

A few things that should be considered and known when it comes to self-love:

You are the main focus – It all starts with you and ends with you. You're going to be with yourself for eternity. This means you want to operate from a place of self-loving rather than self-loathing.

You care for yourself the most – Nobody is interested in you – your well-being, health, safety, happiness, and existence – more than you. No one knows better than you, what makes you happy, or what hurts you most. No one thinks of you or exists ready for your rescue, support, or comfort. No one can make better choices for you or give you a better opinion of what you need to do – other than yourself. No one is here for your spiritual growth – but you.

You are the only person that can bring yourself up or down – You determine your attitude, the way you react, and your outlook day today. This way, if you love yourself, you will be mindful of the way you feel and how you feel it.

❖ What does self-love mean to you?

For starters, it can mean:

- Talking to and about yourself with love
- Prioritizing yourself
- Giving yourself a break from self-judgment
- Trusting yourself
- Being true to yourself
- Being nice to yourself
- Setting healthy boundaries
- Forgiving yourself when you aren't true or nice to yourself
- For many people, self-love is another way to say self-care. To practice self-care, we often need to go back to the basics and Listen to our bodies.
- Take breaks from work and move/stretch.
- Put the phone down and connect to yourself or others, or do something creative.
- Eating healthily, but sometimes indulge in your favorite foods.
- Self-love means accepting yourself as you are in this very moment for everything that you are. It means accepting your emotions for what they are and putting your physical, emotional, and mental well-being first.

❖ How and Why to Practice Self Love

So now we know that self-love motivates you to make healthy choices in life. When you hold yourself in high esteem, you're more likely to choose things that nurture your well-being and serve you well. These things may be in the form of eating healthy, exercising, or having healthy relationships.

❖   Ways to practice self-love include:

**Becoming mindful**. People who have more self-love tend to know what they think, feel, and want.

Taking actions based on need rather than want. By staying focused on what you need, you turn away from automatic behavior patterns that get you into trouble, keep you stuck in the past, and lessen self-love.

**Practicing good self-care**. You will love yourself more when you take better care of your basic needs. People high in self-love nourish themselves daily through healthy activities, like sound nutrition, exercise, proper sleep, intimacy, and healthy social interactions.

**Making room for healthy habits**. Start truly caring for yourself by mirroring that in what you eat, how you exercise, and what you spend time doing. Do stuff, not to "get it done" or because you "have to," but because you care about yourself.

Therapists spend a lot of time talking about self-love. But if you're like many of patients, you might not know what self-love means exactly. Many people mistakenly believe that self-love is the same as narcissism or having a big ego. It's not. So, what do we mean when we say "self-love"? Self-love means having a high regard for your own well-being and happiness. Self-love means taking care of your own needs and not sacrificing your well-being to please others. Self-love means not settling for less than you deserve.

Loving yourself doesn't mean you think you're the smartest, most talented, and most beautiful person in the world. Instead, when you love yourself, you accept your so-called weaknesses, appreciate these so-called shortcomings as something that makes you who you are. When you love yourself, you have compassion for yourself.

You take care of yourself like you'd take care of a friend in distress. You treat yourself kindly. You don't nitpick and criticize yourself. For many, especially those of who grew up in households that lacked love or in which love waxed and waned, loving yourself will take work. Self-love is a practice, and it's a skill that takes work.

Self-love isn't about instant gratification. A new pair of shoes or eating an entire pizza might make you feel good at the moment (or taste delicious), but the feeling isn't lasting–and could be damaging in the long run. Self-love means giving yourself what your body, brain, and soul needs for the marathon that is life. It isn't hedonism, and it isn't chasing a physical or emotional high. The practice of self-love is the practice of nourishing yourself.

Self-love refers to the act of valuing one's own happiness and well-being. Self-love is a kind of acceptance that can be described as an unconditional sense of support and caring and a core of compassion for the self. It might also be considered a willingness to meet personal needs, allow non-judgmental thinking, and view the self as essentially worthy, good, valuable, and deserving of happiness.

Those who find it challenging to practice self-love or have barriers that make it difficult for them to experience compassion or love for themselves may find the support of a therapist or other mental health professional to be beneficial as they explore the reasons behind these difficulties.

❖ WHY IS SELF-LOVE IMPORTANT?

Self-love is considered to be an important component of self-esteem and overall well-being. It is generally difficult, if not impossible, to feel content without first being able to love and accept the self. Researchers have discovered that the practice of self-love is associated with a multitude of benefits, such as greater life satisfaction, increased happiness, and greater resilience.

People with high levels of self-compassion have been shown to often be able to overcome difficult life events, such as divorce, with more ease than those who are harder on themselves. The ability to affirm oneself has also been associated with improved problem-solving abilities and decreased procrastination because it can help individuals recognize the effects of negative habits and behaviors (such as procrastination) without leading to a thought pattern that is excessively negative.

The risk of developing mental health issues such as depression, anxiety, and perfectionism can also be decreased through the practice of self-love. This practice can also increase one's optimism and may be helpful for stress reduction, especially in the face of various life challenges.

Self-love can also lead to improved relationships. The idea that a person should practice self-love before attempting to pursue the love of others is one that is accepted by many, and research has shown that practicing self-love and self-compassion is likely to improve well-being in the context of interpersonal relationships. People who have self-compassion and practice self-love generally report feeling happier and more authentic in their relationships, and thus, they may be better able to assert their needs and opinions. Further, those who practice kindness and compassion on a personal level first may be better able to show kindness and compassion to others and are generally more likely to do so, as the ability to care for and love one's self generally indicates that one will experience a greater capacity to love and care for others.

It is generally considered to be normal for people to have periods in which they feel better about themselves and periods in which confidence and self-esteem wane. After failing at an important task, for example, one may question personal ability and self-worth. Self-love is considered to be an ongoing activity rather than a constant state. For many people, it takes effort, attention, and mindful attempts to practice self-compassion and affirm and accept oneself.

## ❖  CAN SELF-LOVE BE A BAD THING?

Self-love, in this context, can be said to differ from narcissism, as self-love is largely considered to be positive: Self-love is generally beneficial to happiness and well-being, and those who are encouraged to practice self-love may be more likely to achieve and experience success. While narcissism may sometimes be referred to as self-love, narcissism can more accurately be described as excessive self-interest, combined with a general disregard of others and a lack of empathy.

In excess, self-love may become self-centered. A high level of fragile or shallow self-esteem, which may be facilitated by empty praises of well-meaning parents, teachers, or other caregivers during one's childhood, can lead individuals, especially adolescents, to develop traits of narcissism. Research has also shown that inflated self-esteem, which can be linked to excessive self-love, is often associated with cynicism, a lack of motivation, verbal defensiveness, and, in some cases, aggression.

### ❖ SELF-LOVE IN THERAPY

Certain distorted thought processes may make the practice of self-love difficult. Some individuals may believe that they are unworthy of love due to a lack of success in their chosen professional field, for example, or because of certain personal characteristics that they perceive to be negative or flawed. The trouble with relationships or friendships may also lead some to feel as if they may never experience close friendship or love, which can contribute to spiraling negative thoughts that may also have a negative effect on the ability to love the self. Often, cognitive and brief therapies prove helpful, as they focus on correcting these thoughts in order to improve one's ability to love oneself and develop greater self-compassion.

Early experiences such as trauma, abandonment, or neglect can also cause people to feel as if they are unworthy of love. Therapy can help people uncover any possible reasons that it may be difficult to practice self-love. In therapy, people seeking treatment may become better able to understand the ways that early experiences still affect them and, with the help of a therapist, may be able to overcome past trauma and any feelings of self-loathing.

Therapy can also provide a space where one feels loved and accepted. The concept of unconditional positive regard, initially developed by Carl Rogers and used in person-centered (Rogerian) therapy, holds that providing a relationship in which one is truly accepted, without any conditions or judgment, allows healing to occur, in most cases. By providing unconditional positive regard, a therapist can also help people in therapy to learn to harbor that degree of love and acceptance toward themselves. For individuals who have never experienced love or acceptance and find it difficult to practice self-love. As a result, this therapeutic bond may foster the development of self-compassion and love, leading to a state of improved mental health.

### ❖ CULTURAL DIFFERENCES OF SELF-LOVE

The expression of self-love can change depending on cultural context, though self-love appears to represent an important aspect of human existence. People from some cultures may be less likely to speak positively about themselves, especially to others in spheres outside those of close friends and family, as in these cultures, modesty and humility may be more valued. One study found that although people from some East Asian cultures were found to love and feel as good about themselves as did the Americans also surveyed, those from East Asian cultures evaluated themselves less positively on a cognitive level.

### ❖ WHAT IS SELF-CONFIDENCE?

Confidence can be a tough thing to build up. We've put together some handy tips to help you out. If you're still having a hard time even after trying these self-help ideas, don't worry! We've also listed the ways you can find extra support and work on boosting your confidence with the help of others.

### ❖ What is a confident person?

Not everyone is born with an inbuilt sense of self-confidence. Sometimes it can be hard to develop confidence, either because personal experiences have caused you to lose confidence or because you suffer from low self-esteem.

A confident person:

- Does what they believe is right, even if it's unpopular

- Is willing to take risks
- Admits their mistakes and learns from them
- Is able to accept a compliment
- Is optimistic.

Self-confidence is an attitude about your skills and abilities. It means you accept and trust yourself and have a sense of control in your life. You know your strengths and weakness well and have a positive view of yourself. You set realistic expectations and goals, communicate assertively, and can handle criticism.

On the other hand, low self-confidence might make you feel full of self-doubt, be passive or submissive, or have difficulty trusting others. You may feel inferior, unloved, or be sensitive to criticism. Feeling confident in yourself might depend on the situation. For instance, you can feel very confident in some areas, such as academics, but lack confidence in others, like relationships.

Having high or low self-confidence is rarely related to your actual abilities and mostly based on your perceptions. Perceptions are the way your think about yourself, and these thoughts can be flawed.

Low self-confidence might stem from different experiences, such as growing up in an unsupportive and critical environment, being separated from your friends or family for the first time, judging yourself too harshly, or being afraid of failure. People with low self-confidence often have errors in their thinking.

❖ How To Increase Your Self-Confidence

- Recognize and emphasize your strengths. Reward and

praise yourself for your efforts and progress.
- When you stumble on an obstacle, treat yourself with kindness and compassion. Don't dwell on failure.
- Set realistic and achievable goals. Do not expect perfection; it is impossible to be perfect in every aspect of life.
- Slow down when you are feeling intense emotions and think logically about the situation.
- Challenge making assumptions about yourself, people, and situations.
- Recognize that past negative life experiences do not dictate your future.
- Express your feelings, beliefs, and needs directly and respectfully
- Learn to say no to unreasonable requests.

There are a number of things you can do to build your confidence. Some of them are just small changes to your frame of mind; others you'll have to work on for a bit longer to make them familiar habits.

## 1. Look at what you've already achieved

It's easy to lose confidence if you believe you haven't achieved anything. Make a list of all the things you're proud of in your life, whether it's getting a good mark on an exam or learning to surf. Keep the list close by and add to it whenever you do something you're proud of. When you're low in confidence, pull out the list and use it to remind yourself of all the awesome stuff you've done.

## 2. Think of things you're good at

Everyone has strengths and talents. What are yours? Recognizing what you're good at, and trying to build on those things, will help you to build confidence in your own abilities.

### 3. Set some goals

Set some goals and set out the steps you need to take to achieve them. They don't have to be big goals; they can even be things like baking a cake or planning a night out with friends. Just aim for some small achievements that you can tick off a list to help you gain confidence in your ability to get stuff done.

### 4. Talk yourself up

You're never going to feel confident if you have negative commentary running through your mind telling you that you're no good. Think about your self-talk and how that might be affecting your self-confidence. Treat yourself like you would your best friend and cheer yourself on.

### 5. Get a hobby

Try to find something that you're really passionate about. It could be photography, sport, knitting, or anything else! When you've worked out your passion, commit yourself to give it a go. Chances are, if you're interested or passionate about a certain activity, you're more likely to be motivated, and you'll build skills more quickly.

- Building up a good sense of self-esteem is helpful for adolescents to
- Enhance their psycho-social health. Self-esteem is a person's
- Subjective evaluation of his or her own worth; it serves as an Important index of a person's psychological health

and will affect a person's behaviors.
- People with higher self-esteem are more able to recognize their values and strengths and accept their weaknesses at the same time.
- In general, people with higher self-esteem are more confident across different aspects.

Many factors can affect our self-esteem. For example, one's genetic makeup, personality, family, school, and peers are all important elements. Evaluations from parents, teachers, schoolmates, and friends can affect the ways how we perceive ourselves, which then gradually build up our self-esteem.

- Do you like yourself?
- Are you satisfied with yourself?
- Are you willing to improve your weaknesses?
- Do you think you are useless?
- Do you think you are unlikable?
- Do you often think you are inferior to others?
- Do you have the confidence to achieve your goals?
- Do you refuse to try due to fear of failure?

The above questions help us to evaluate our self-esteem. Our self-esteem will be higher if the answers of the above tend to be positive.

We fail to do some things like;

## 1. Appreciate yourselves

You can write a list of your strengths and Ways to cultivate better self-esteem Ways to cultivate better self-esteem achievements (e.g., you are honest, sincere to others, or good at sport, etc.)

You may then put the list in some conspicuous place, ascertain your own strengths and keep it up.

## 2. Recognize your value

All things in their being are good for something. We are sure to say: "I am a valuable person." Everyone is unique, and we should live with self-respect. Equip ourselves and contribute to our family, school, and community.

## 3. Accept ourselves and build up positive self-images

Adolescents need to accept their appearance and personal background, and recognize the values of one's inner strengths and virtues. We can learn from others' good behaviors and build up better self-images.

## 4. Develop and make good use of our potential

Explore our potential by joining various kinds of extra-curricular activities. For example, scout association, outward bound training, various interest groups, and voluntary community services

are good ways to explore and develop our potential interests and abilities

## 5. Improve our weaknesses

No one is perfect, and we should not look down upon ourselves due to weaknesses in some aspects. We should have reasonable expectations and set achievable goals according to our abilities. We should keep improving our weaknesses by persistently adhering to our plans

## 6. Do not compare with others

There is always someone better than you. Comparing with others is endless, and this can hurt your self-esteem. Setting attainable goals and putting persistent effort to improve ourselves is more under our own control.

## 7. Do not give up but shape up

Do not see yourselves as losers even when you fail. We can learn from mistakes, evaluate both external and internal factors, improve those we can change, and strive to get better results for the coming challenges.

## 8. Correct mistakes, rebuild self-esteem

Everyone makes mistakes. It is more important to learn from our weaknesses, and preventing them from happening again can help to improve our self-esteem.

## 9. Love ourselves

Take good care of ourselves and live healthily. Live our lives to the fullest and avoid harmful behaviors

such as smoking, taking drugs, or committing offenses, etc

## 10. Build up a social network and make appropriate use of it

Build up mutual respect and trust with your parents, another family members, teachers, and friends in our daily lives. We can share our difficulties to them and obtain their advice and support

# HOW TO STOP OVERTHINKING

*"Those only are happy (I thought) who have their minds fixed on some object other than their own happiness; on the happiness of others, on the improvement of mankind, even on some art or pursuit, followed not as a means, but as itself an ideal end. Aiming thus at something else, they find happiness by the way. The enjoyments of life (such was now my theory) are sufficient to make it a pleasant thing, when they are taken en passant, without being made a principal object. Once make them so, and they are immediately felt to be insufficient. They will not bear a scrutinizing examination. Ask yourself whether you are happy, and you cease to be so. The only chance is to treat, not happiness, but some end external to it, as the purpose of life. Let your self-consciousness, your scrutiny, your self-interrogation, exhaust themselves on that; and if otherwise fortunately circumstanced you will inhale happiness with the air you breathe, without dwelling on it or thinking about it, without either forestalling it in imagination, or putting it to flight by fatal questioning—John Stuart Mill,*

The classic overthinking definition is "to think about something too much or for too long." While it's human nature to think things through when making a decision or evaluating a situation, it becomes overthinking when you can't get out of your own head. It happens to all of us at some point in our lives – we all experience events that cause us to worry or stress. But some people can't seem to turn their concerns off. They worry about the future, making catastrophic predictions about unlikely events that haven't happened yet. They also ruminate about the past, beating themselves up about "should haves" and "could haves." They fret over what others might think of them or let negative self-talk build up in their minds.

**Overthinking is exhausting.**

When you overthink, thoughts run circles around your head, and you find yourself stuck in reverse, unable to move forward. More so, you start coming up with bizarre ideas that totally contradict each other.

*"I'm so excited for this job interview" transforms into "I wonder if they liked me" and then morphs into "oh, I'm so stupid! I shouldn't have said that! I'm definitely not getting an offer."*

You start blaming yourself for things you didn't do and worrying about scenarios that may or may not happen.

Overthinking is simply the act of "thinking about something too much or for too long."

know the feeling, and it's energy-draining. In fact, studies have shown that overthinking elevates your stress levels, reduces your creativity, clouds your judgment, and strips of your power to make decisions.

Overthinking a tough decision you have to make can also cause problems. Replaying all the options in your head can lead to "paralysis by analysis" – you're afraid to take the wrong action, so you take no action at all. But even making the wrong decision is better than making no decision.

Whether you're a chronic overthinker or need to make a tough decision, you've probably experienced sleepless nights when your brain just won't turn off. Overthinking can increase symptoms of depression, elevate your stress levels, and cloud your judgment.

❖ How to Know When You're Overthinking

Thinking about all the things you could have done differently, second-guessing every decision you make, and imagining all the worst-case scenarios in life can be exhausting. But, overthinking is a hard habit to break.

You might even convince yourself that thinking about something for a really long time is the key to developing the best solution, but that's usually not the case.

In fact, the longer you think about something, the less time and energy you might have to take productive action.

Of course, everyone overthinks sometimes. Maybe you keep thinking about all the things that could go wrong when you give a presentation next week.

Maybe you've wasted countless hours trying to decide what to wear to that job interview, and as a result, you didn't spend any time preparing your answers.

Before you can put an end to overthinking, you have to recognize when you're doing it. Here's how to know when you're overthinking.

**You're Not Solution-Focused**

Overthinking is different from problem-solving. Overthinking is about dwelling on the problem, while problem-solving involves looking for a solution.

Imagine a storm is coming. Here's the difference between

overthinking and problem-solving:

**Overthinking:** "I wish the storm wouldn't come. It's going to be awful. I hope the house doesn't get damaged. Why do these things always have to happen to me? I can't handle this."

**Problem-solving**: "I will go outside and pick up everything that might blow away. I'll put sandbags against the garage door to prevent flooding. If we get a lot of rain I'll go to the store to buy plywood so I can board up the windows."

Problem-solving can lead to productive action. Overthinking, on the other hand, fuels uncomfortable emotions and doesn't look for solutions.

**You Experience Repetitive Thoughts**

Ruminating—or rehashing the same things over and over again —isn't helpful. But, when you're overthinking, you might find yourself replaying a conversation in your head repeatedly or imagining something bad happening many times.

**Your Worrying Keeps You Up at Night**

When you're overthinking, you might feel like your brain won't shut off. When you try to sleep, you might even feel as though your brain is on overdrive as it replays scenarios in your head and causes you to imagine bad things happening.

Research confirms what you likely already know—rumination interferes with sleep. Overthinking makes it harder to fall asleep.

Overthinking impairs the quality of your sleep too. So it's harder to fall into a deep slumber when your brain is busy overthinking everything.

Difficulty falling asleep may contribute to more worrisome thoughts. For example, when you don't fall asleep right away, you might imagine that you'll be overtired the following day. That may cause you to feel anxious—which may make it even harder to fall asleep.

## You Struggle to Make Decisions

You might try to convince yourself that thinking longer and harder helps you. After all, you're looking at a problem from every possible angle.

But, overanalyzing and obsessing actually becomes a barrier. Research shows thinking too much makes it tough to make decisions.

If you're indecisive about everything from what to eat for dinner to which hotel you should book, you might be overthinking things.

It's very likely that you are wasting a lot of time looking for second opinions and researching your options when ultimately, those little choices might not matter so much.

## You Second Guess Decisions

Overthinking sometimes involves beating yourself up for the decisions you already made.

You could waste a lot of time thinking your life would be better if you'd only taken that other job or not started a business. Or maybe you get upset with yourself for not seeing red flags sooner because you believe they should have been obvious!

And while a little healthy self-reflection can help you learn from your mistakes, rehashing and second-guessing is a form of mental torture.

Overthinking can take a toll on your mood and may make it even more difficult to make decisions in the future.

**What to Do About Overthinking**

Research shows thinking less about a problem might actually be the key to developing better solutions. Studies show an "incubation period" may help you make the best decisions.

- Distracting Yourself Can Help

Rather than sit and think about a problem for endless amounts of time, you can distract yourself for a bit.

Your brain may find better ways to work out a solution in the background while you're distracted by another task like working in the garden. Or, you might "sleep on it" and discover that your brain solves the problem for you while you're sleeping.

A brief distraction can give you a break. And it may get your mind focused on something more productive. And, your brain might even develop a solution for you when you stop thinking about the problem.

Would people call you a "worrier?" Are your fingernails bitten down to little nubs because you're constantly thinking about the general "what its" of life?

Think about how much you're missing out on because of worry. Does it take you away from fun social events? Does it impact your performance at work? Does it keep you from getting close to someone in a new relationship? How could have simple resources at your fingertips to stop overthinking so much impact your life for the better?

Worrying itself isn't a disease. In fact, it's a problem a lot of people face. But when you let overthinking take over your life, it can eventually turn into anxiety.

**So, how to stop overthinking?**

There are things you can do to stop overthinking about every little thing — That doesn't mean you ignore the hard stuff. It means you can take a breath and relax a bit more!

Of course, it takes practice and time to stop overthinking after years of making it a habit.

By utilizing some of the tips listed here, you can start to find some peace and freedom from the things that plague your thoughts each day.

- Realize You're Doing It

The first step in putting a stop to overthinking about everything is to acknowledge that you're a worrier. Think it sounds easy? Not exactly.

It's hard for us, as human beings, to admit we've got a problem — big or small. However, realizing that you overthink things is the only way you'll even have a desire to put a stop to it or make a change.

The next time you catch yourself worrying about something, pump the brakes. You don't have to dig into the underlying cause of that worry just yet. Instead, acknowledge the fact that you might be overthinking the subject.

That simple "pause" and acknowledgment can help you come back to the reality of the situation and make it feel less scary and overwhelming.

- See the World — or At Least Your Community

Did you know that travel is scientifically proven to ease anxiety, stress, and depression? Sounds like a perfect excuse to buy that plane ticket and plan a trip to go backpacking in Europe.

Traveling can help to give you a new perspective on life. It also gives you something to look forward to, which can be a welcomed distraction from your worries.

To put it simply: a holiday can make you happier. Been found that people who know they have a vacation coming up are happier.

It also helps to give your brainpower a boost and increases your overall satisfaction with life. More satisfaction means less time to worry!

The good news? You don't necessarily have to leave the country or even your state to take advantage of the benefits of travel. Explore your community, spend a night at a local bed and breakfast, take a staycation or take part in a local tourist attraction you've never seen before.

- Don't Believe Every Thought

Don't believe the lies your own mind tells you.

It seems like a simple enough statement, but it's hard to do for people who are chronic worriers or who tend to overthink everything.

The truth is, you have the power to take control of your thoughts. When negative self-talk creeps in, you don't have to believe it. You can acknowledge it — and you should. But you have a choice on whether you let it take over. Just because your own mind is telling you to overthink something or be fearful about something doesn't mean you have to.

Interesting concept, isn't it? The best part is, you can put this tip into practice every time worry tries to slither its way in and ruin your day.

- Distract Yourself

You can distract yourself from yourself.

When you overthink things, those thoughts and worries start to take over your mind. You can fight back against them by immediately doing something else that engages your brain.

This could include writing in a journal, doing twenty pushups, reading a book, or calling up your best friend. Whatever you can do to get yourself out of that moment of worry, take action and do it.

You might be surprised at how quickly the thoughts pass through when you don't give them the power to take over.

- Confuse Your Senses

Overthinking and worrying are mental activities, so if they start to take hold, do something physical.

You can essentially "shock" your senses by taking power away from one area of your body and giving it to another. Sounds confusing? It's not.

For example, if you start to feel fearful about the uncertainty of an upcoming event, splash some cold water on your face, or smell some calming lavender oils. Your brain will start to react to the sudden change, and you'll have less of an ability to focus on the worrisome thoughts.

Find whatever works for you to shock your senses, and keep it handy whenever possible.

- Don't Sweat the Small Stuff

You've probably heard this expression before, but when you're an over-thinker, you should really take it to heart.

There are things in life you're going to be able to control and things you can't. Recognize the things you can't control and accept them for what they are.

That means you're going to have to let some things go. It'll take time and practice, but the more aware you are of the things you can't control, the easier it will eventually become to stop fretting about them so much.

- Go Easy on Yourself

You're not perfect, and you don't have to be.

That's more than a motivational speech; it's a reality. Perfectionism is often linked with overthinking and anxiety, but the two actually work in a vicious cycle. People often pursue perfection in order to deal with worry and anxiety, but that tends to make them even more anxious because it's impossible to be perfect.

It's not easy to admit and accept imperfections, but when you realize no one is perfect, you can take baby steps toward letting go of your worrying thoughts and give yourself some slack.

- Take a Picture, It Lasts Longer

Photography, especially nature and landscape photography, can reduce stress and help to distract you from your own worries and overthinking.

Why does it work? When you're taking photographs, you're in the present moment. You're mindful of the world around you and what you're viewing through a screen. You won't have time to worry because your mind isn't allowed to wander to your past or future, at least for a few moments.

Photography also allows you to open up your creative side, which is a stress-reducer, and a way to find more balance each day. You don't have to become a professional — just find what inspires you and start snapping!

- Get Your Hands Dirty

You don't have to have a green thumb in order to take advantage of the benefits of gardening.

Today, gardening can provide you with mental health benefits like relaxation and mindfulness. It allows you to vent your worries, your aggressions, and even your excessive thoughts. It also gives you a healthy sense of control, which can offer a nice balance for someone who tends to think too much.

If you're new to the gardening game, start small and use some simple hacks, so you don't get overwhelmed. Plant some seedlings in eggshells to get them started, and use cooking water on your plants as a natural fertilizer.

Before you know it, you'll have a beautiful garden from all of your efforts and an outlet to dig your worries away.

- Listen to Music

Turn up the radio, put your headphones in, and blast your favorite tunes.

Music has many healing properties and psychological benefits. It can improve your concentration, reduce stress, and give your memory a boost.

Music can also help you to be more self-aware, which makes it easier to identify overthinking habits. When you're actively engaged in listening or playing music, you're more mindful of the moment and less worried about everything else.

Choosing to listen to music also offers a welcomed distraction, which brings us to our next point.

- Get Up and Get Moving

Sometimes, sweat can be the best cure for a worried mind.

There are so many benefits to exercise, including a boost in your cardiovascular health and an improvement in mood. Aside from being a part of a healthy lifestyle, exercise also has psychological benefits.

Exercise allows you to set goals, which will keep you focused (and distracted from worries). You'll also achieve a sense of accomplishment when you reach those goals. So, not only are you doing something good for your body, but you're giving your brain a boost and kicking your worries to the curb in the process.

Bonus points: choose to exercise outside as spending time in nature has its own mood-boosting benefits![5]

- Build a Budget

One of life's biggest stressors is money.

In fact, according to a study by Northwestern Mutual, it's the number one source of stress for Americans. On the flip side, the same study also found that most people feel happier and more confident when they know they've got a handle on their finances.

If one of your major worries involves how much money you have, a simple solution is to pay more attention to it. Creating a budget, especially for a growing family, allows you to better identify your spending habits and decide where you can cut back and what your financial priorities really are.

Money might be a major worry for some people, but with a little extra time and planning, you can get it under control to the point where you'll hardly ever have to think about it.

- Practice Meditation

Meditation has been stereotyped into a corner for years, but it doesn't have to be what you see in the movies

Meditation is simply a relaxation technique that allows you to be mindful and focused on the present moment rather than letting your anxious thoughts take over.

You don't have to practice any special rituals in order to meditate. Finding just a few minutes a day to sit in silence, focus on your breathing, and let thoughts come and go freely can make a big difference in the overall health of your mental state.

It can take practice to clear your head, even for a few minutes, but try to make meditation a part of your daily routine, and you'll undoubtedly start to recognize the calming effects it can have.

- Practice Gratitude

Having an attitude of gratitude is more than just a cheesy saying they told you at summer camp — it's a necessity for someone who overthinks everything.

The benefits of gratitude range from physical to psychological. It can improve your self-esteem and increase your overall mental strength.

By keeping a daily journal of things you're grateful for, you'll have something to reference and look back on in moments that feel overwhelming or when you find yourself drowning with worry. Gratitude can give you a different perspective on things, so the situations you're overthinking about become less important.

- Understand What Motivates Your Worry

Have you ever wondered why you overthink and worry so much?

If you take the time to think about it, there might be some underlying causes as to why you struggle so much with excessive worry.

It's not easy to face your fears, but it's also not easy to face what might be causing those fears. Find some time and a safe space where you can really look inside yourself to better understand your motivations, so you can take control of them and possibly get the help you need to get rid of them.

It's not always easy to take back your freedom from fear, but it's not impossible.

**Short Breathing Exercise On How To Overcome Overthinking**

1. Lengthen your exhale

Inhaling deeply may not always calm you down. Taking a deep breath in is actually linked to the sympathetic nervous system, which controls the fight-or-flight response. But exhaling is linked to the parasympathetic nervous system, which influences our body's ability to relax and calm down.

Taking too many deep breaths too quickly can actually cause you to hyperventilate. Hyperventilation decreases the amount of oxygen-rich blood that flows to your brain.

When we feel anxious or under stress, it's easier to breathe too much and end up hyperventilating — even if we're trying to do the opposite.

- Before you take a big, deep breath, try a thorough exhale instead. Push all the air out of your lungs, then simply let your lungs do their work inhaling air.
- Next, try spending a little bit longer exhaling than you do inhaling. For example, try inhaling for four seconds, then exhale for six.
- Try doing this for two to five minutes.

This technique can be done in any position that's comfortable for you, including standing, sitting, or lying down.

2. Abdomen breathing

Breathing from your diaphragm (the muscle that sits just beneath your lungs) can help reduce the amount of work your body needs to do in order to breathe.

To learn how to breathe from your diaphragm:

Check-in

- For comfort, lie down on the floor or bed with pillows beneath your head and knees. Or sit in a comfortable chair with your head, neck, and shoulders relaxed and your knees bent.
- Then, put one hand under your rib cage and one hand over your heart.
- Inhale and exhale through your nose, noticing how or if your stomach and chest move as you breathe.
- Can you isolate your breathing, so you bring air deeper into your lungs? What about the reverse? Can you breathe so your chest moves more than your stomach?

Eventually, you want your stomach to move as you breathe instead of your chest.

Practice belly breathing

- Sit or lie down as described above.
- Place one hand on your chest and one hand on your stomach somewhere above your belly button.
- Breathe in through your nose, noticing your stomach rise. Your chest should remain relatively still.

4.        Purse your lips and exhale through your mouth. Try engaging your stomach muscles to push air out at the end of the breath.

For this type of breathing to become automatic, you'll need to practice it daily. Try doing the exercise three or four times a day for up to 10 minutes.

If you haven't been using your diaphragm to breathe, you may feel tired at first. It'll get easier with practice, though.

## 3. Breath focus

When deep breathing is focused and slow, it can help reduce anxiety. You can do this technique by sitting or lying down in a quiet, comfortable location. Then:

- Notice how it feels when you inhale and exhale normally. Mentally scan your body. You might feel the tension in your body that you never noticed.
- Take a slow, deep breath through your nose.
- Notice your belly and upper body expanding.
- Exhale in whatever way is most comfortable for you, sighing if you wish.
- Do this for several minutes, paying attention to the rise and fall of your belly.
- Choose a word to focus on and vocalize during your exhale. Words like "safe" and "calm" can be effective.
- Imagine your inhale washing over you like a gentle wave.
- Imagine your exhale carrying negative and upsetting thoughts and energy away from you.
- When you get distracted, gently bring your attention back to your breath and your words.

Practice this technique for up to 20 minutes daily when you can.

## 4. Equal breathing

Another form of breathing that stems from the ancient practice of pranayama yoga is equal breathing. This means you're inhaling for the same amount of time as you're exhaling.

You can practice equal breathing from a sitting or lying-down position. Whichever position you choose, be sure to get comfortable.

- Shut your eyes and pay attention to the way you

> normally breathe for several breaths.
- Then, slowly count 1-2-3-4 as you inhale through your nose.
- Exhale for the same four-second count.
- As you inhale and exhale, be mindful of the feelings of fullness and emptiness in your lungs.

As you continue practicing equal breathing, your second count might vary. Be sure to keep your inhale and exhale the same.

5. Resonant breathing

Resonant breathing, also called coherent breathing, can help you calm anxiety and get into a relaxed state. To try it yourself:

- Lie down and close your eyes.
- Gently breathe in through your nose, mouth closed, for a count of six seconds.
- Don't fill your lungs too full of air.
- Exhale for six seconds, allowing your breath to leave your body slowly and gently. Don't force it.
- Continue for up to 10 minutes.
- Take a few additional minutes to be still and focus on how your body feels.

Yogic breathing (pranayama)

Yoga is a wellness practice with ancient roots, and breathing is at the heart of each variation of yoga.

One form of yoga, pranayama, includes multiple breathing variations that may help with anxiety. Some of these include lengthened exhale and equal breathing (both featured above), as well as lion's breath and alternate nostril breathing

6. Lion's breath

Lion's breath involves exhaling forcefully. To try lion's breath:

- Get into a kneeling position, crossing your ankles and resting your bottom on your feet. If this position isn't comfortable, sit cross-legged.

- Bring your hands to your knees, stretching out your arms and your fingers.
- Take a breath in through your nose.
- Breathe out through your mouth, allowing yourself to vocalize "ha."
- During exhale, open your mouth as wide as you can and stick your tongue out, stretching it down toward your chin as far as it will go.
- Focus on the middle of your forehead (third eye) or the end of your nose while exhaling.
- Relax your face as you inhale again.
- Repeat the practice up to six times, changing the cross of your ankles when you reach the halfway point.

7. Alternate nostril breathing

To try alternate nostril breathing, sit down in a comfortable place, lengthening your spine and opening your chest.

Rest your left hand in your lap and raise your right hand. Then, rest the pointer and middle fingers of your right hand on your forehead, in between the eyebrows. Close your eyes, inhaling and exhaling through your nose.

- Use your right thumb to close the right-hand nostril and inhale slowly through the left.
- Pinch your nose closed between your right thumb and ring finger, holding the breath in for a moment.
- Use your right ring finger to close your left nostril and exhale through the right, waiting for a moment before you inhale again.
- Inhale slowly through the right nostril.
- Pinch your nose closed again, pausing for a moment.
- Now, open the left side and exhale, waiting a moment before you inhale again.
- Repeat this cycle of inhaling and exhaling through either nostril up to 10 times. Each cycle should take up to 40 seconds.

## 8. Guided meditation

Some people use guided meditation to alleviate anxiety by interrupting patterns of thinking that perpetuate stress.

You can practice guided meditation by sitting or lying in a cool, dark, comfortable place and relaxing. Then, listen to calming recordings while relaxing your body and steadying your breathing.

Guided meditation recordings help take you through the steps of visualizing a calmer, less stressed reality. It can also help you gain control over intrusive thoughts that trigger anxiety.

Meditation can help you establish new habits and patterns of thinking. If you'd like to try it yourself, UCLA has guided meditation recordings available for streaming here.

**The takeaway**

If you're experiencing anxiety or panic attacks, try using one or more of these breathing techniques to see if they can alleviate your symptoms.

If your anxiety persists or gets worse, make an appointment with your doctor to discuss your symptoms and possible treatments. With the right approach, you can regain your quality of life and control over your anxiety.

# HOW TO OVERCOME NEGATIVITY

*"With everything that has happened to you, you can either feel sorry for yourself or treat what has happened as a gift. Everything is either an opportunity to grow or an obstacle to keep you from growing. You get to choose." – Dr. Wayne Dyer.*

Do you ever struggle with negative thinking? If you have a harsh inner critic or get caught in worry, stress, anxiety, depression, or wrestle with low self-worth, then you know some of the symptoms first hand.

Negative (unhelpful) thinking patterns can have a strong and sometimes devastating impact on our relationships, our health, our work… our lives.

❖ INEFFECTIVE WAYS PEOPLE TRY TO STOP NEGATIVE THINKING

People often try many different ways to get rid of their negative thoughts, including distractions, diversions, or 'drowning their sorrows,' only to later mentally beat themselves up for being still stuck in their negativity. It can feel like a real internal battle. These are common strategies that attempt to stop the thoughts and numb the pain in the short term, but they only make things worse in the long term. It doesn't fix the problem at its core.

**THE FOUR KEYS TO OVERCOMING NEGATIVE THINKING**

❖　　KEY ONE: RECOGNISE & STEP BACK FROM NEGATIVE THOUGHT PATTERNS

Negative thought patterns are repetitive, unhelpful thoughts. They directly cause what we could describe as 'negative' (unwanted or unpleasant) emotions like anxiety, depression, stress, fear, unworthiness, shame, etc.

Once we learn to recognize and identify negative thought patterns as they occur, we can start to step back from them. This process of stepping back from thoughts is called 'cognitive defusion.' In cognitive defusion, we learn to see the thoughts in our head as simply that—just thoughts. Not reality. You see, when we are fused with our thoughts (cognitive fusion), we tend to take our thoughts very, very seriously. We believe them. We buy into them, and we obey them. We play them out.

When we are not fused with our thoughts—when we can step back into cognitive defusion, we do not take our thoughts too seriously. We hold them lightly. We only listen to them if we find them valuable or helpful. We certainly don't take our thoughts to be 'the truth,' and we don't automatically obey them or play them out. We see our thoughts as simply bits of language that pass through the mind. Mental events, if you will, that move through the mind all the time just like the weather passes through the sky. We have a choice in how we choose to respond to them.

Will like to use the example to illustrate the difference between cognitive fusion, and cognitive defusion is…imagining waking up one day and looking out the window and seeing rain. A thought might come into your head that says, "what a dreadful day." Now is it true that the day is dreadful? No, of course not; it is simply raining. However, if you believe the thought "what a dreadful day," in other words, if you are stuck in cognitive fusion (literally fused with the thought), then guess what you will probably have? That's right; you will probably have a dreadful day! In other words, if you believe a thought like that, it can generate what we might call negativity.

It's completely normal to have negative thoughts! It's part of our evolutionary history. There is nothing wrong with you. We all have minds that have evolved to be constantly on the lookout for problems and dangers, so most of us have minds prone to have many negative thoughts.

The problem is not that we have negative thoughts. The problem comes when we believe our thoughts are true. When you are no longer entangled in thoughts, they lose their grip on you and lose their power to generate unpleasant emotions.

Let's go back to the example above. Imagine you're laying in bed in the morning, you look out the window, and you see that it's raining, and once again, the thought arises, "what a dreadful day." If you are not fused with the thought (you don't buy into it), your experience would be like this. You're watching the rain falling, then you also watch the thought (as simply a mental event) "what a dreadful day" arise and fall away just like the rain is falling... and since you don't take it seriously or believe it, it generates no negativity, passes by easily and you're free to lay there relaxed and at ease, enjoying the pitter-patter of the rain on the roof.

As you can see, the ability to recognize unhelpful thinking and step back from it is incredibly liberating! It can change the quality of your whole day and indeed your whole life.

It's important to recognize the kinds of unhelpful thinking styles that can arise, so here are some other negative thinking patterns that are most common. Be on the lookout for them, and below,

## ANXIOUS THOUGHTS AND WORRY

Worry is when the mind projects into an imagined future and conjures up scenes and thoughts about what could go wrong. Here it often creates 'what if' scenarios.

Sometimes it takes the form of imagining or expecting that bad things will happen or that nothing good will ever happen for you. You might fret about your health deteriorating, your relationship going downhill, your car breaking down, or your career being ruined—even though nothing has happened yet.

You might focus on the lack in your life and believe that nothing will ever get better for you. Stress-related to your financial future, your children's welfare, or your partner leaving you fit into this category.

## CRITICISM AND SELF-BEATING

Do you have a harsh inner critic? Are you always trying to whip yourself into shape, mentally beating yourself up for not being good enough yet? Are you on a perfect mission? Another negative thought pattern is to constantly criticize and 'self improve' because you're not good enough yet. You may be very harsh on yourself, focusing on all of your weaknesses and perceived flaws.

Likewise, you may extend this habit of criticism to others in your life. This can be the cause of tremendous strain on relationships. Negative self-talk and self-criticism often result in low self-esteem and a lack of confidence.

Some people cope with low self-esteem to compensate for these feelings by attaining status, achievements, and recognition.

Others may feel completely debilitated by feelings of unworthiness, becoming depressed, or even suicidal.

There is nothing wrong with having goals and aiming to get fitter or healthier and the like—we can simply choose to do those because they are good for us or want to stretch and grow. It's a very different headspace to be doing those things because we don't feel like we're enough yet.

When the mind continuously hones in on what is wrong with yourself (and your life) and disassociates from what is going well and is good, we can become stuck in negativity.

## REGRET AND GUILT

Ruminating on mistakes made in the past often creates feelings of shame, guilt, and negativity. Feelings of worthlessness may arise when you repeatedly play in your mind 'bad' choices or 'wrong' actions you feel you have made.

There is nothing 'negative' per set about simply reflecting on past experiences. This is how we can learn, grow and mature as people. Negativity arises when you dwell on a situation repeatedly with no real intention to learn and grow–but instead, you are self-beating or wishing things were different instead of accepting things as they are.

## PROBLEMS

Negative thoughts often revolve around what's wrong with your life. Your attention becomes fixated on and exaggerates the so-called negative aspects of your life. Here your mind will often downplay what is going well.

For example, you may have a wonderful family, food to eat, and shelter, but your car breaks down, and it's all you can think about and focus on all week long. You allow the car to dominate your thinking, and negative emotions arise as a result.

All week you are frustrated, angry, and depressed because of the car when your focus could be expanded to what is going well and what you're grateful for.

The truth is that the car has a problem. It is no longer running and needs to be taken to the mechanic. That's a simple fact. Ruminating continuously on the situation is not constructive and is another way we can get trapped in negativity.

If you have this habit of lamenting over your sorrows and problems, you may constantly feel frustrated, anxious, depressed, and apathetic. When you're so absorbed in what's wrong, you're unable to notice what's right.

Looking out for and recognizing these common negative thinking patterns when they arise will help you know when to use the tools below to work with them skillfully and break free from their grip.

**GETTING UNSTUCK: THE 'NAME IT TO TAME IT' TECHNIQUE**

People trapped in negative thinking often tell me they feel hopeless because they often wrestle or argue with the thoughts or push them away, but the research shows that trying to struggle with thoughts in these ways just amplifies them, as you may have noticed in your own life. What you resist persists.

❖  KEY TWO: COMING TO YOUR SENSES

*"Let us not look back in anger or forward in fear, but around in awareness." ~ James Thurber*

Notice that many negative thoughts mostly flow from two directions. The first is dwelling on the past—maybe you ruminate over mistakes, problems, guilt, and anything in your life that's did not go the way you believe it should have gone. The second is worrying about the future—fear of what may or may not happen for yourself, others, or the planet.

This may take the form of stress over whether or not you will achieve certain goals or anxiety about the security of your finances or relationships. Or perhaps you may worry about getting old. Whatever your particular negative thoughts are, notice that to engage in negative thought patterns, the mind needs to cast its focus mostly on the past or future. Either that or we judge and mentally label things in the present moment to be 'bad.'

When lost in negative thinking, we tend to be so engrossed in thoughts that we completely lose touch with what is happening in the present moments of our lives. We miss the little pleasures of living each day. The sunlight on your skin, the taste of the food we're eating, a real connection with someone we love while they are talking. When we're lost on our heads, we lose touch with the world around us….and we lose touch with ourselves.

One powerful method is to come to your senses to become more present and able to step out of negative thinking. To do this, simply redirect your attention out of the thoughts in your head and bring your focus to your sense perceptions.

Whether you're in your home, at the office, in the park, or on a subway, notice everything around you. Use your senses to their fullest. Don't get into a mental dialogue about the things you see; just be aware of what you're experiencing at this moment.

### ❖ KEY THREE: REGULAR MINDFULNESS PRACTICE

At the core of each one of us is a space that knows deep peace. As we grow up, we tend to get more and more drawn into the mind – our problems, our goals, our hopes, our fears, and desires. We tend to get so busy, caught up, and lose touch with this deeper sense of self...this pure unconditioned awareness.

It becomes easy for us to get more drawn into negative thinking the more we lose touch with ourselves in this way and lose ourselves in mind.

Mindfulness is the practice of waking up to that wellspring of wholeness and peace. It's waking up out of mind wandering (where we are lost in our heads, our old beliefs, habits, reactions, and thinking patterns) so that we can live deliberately. Through mindfulness, we build our capacity to live from that deeper awareness and tame the mind.

**Four Ways You're Strengthening Your Mind When You Practice Meditation:**

Each time your mind wanders in meditation, your task is to notice it and then detach from your thought stream and come back to your senses at the moment. This is a practice of untangling from thoughts over and over again, a habit which translates in the rest of your life too. It becomes a habit to notice and let go with ease.

Each time you let go of the thought stream and come back into the present moment, you tap into the stillness and wholeness at the heart of who you are. A sense of peace, lightness, and joy arises more and more with each time you practice.

Each time you are kind and gentle with yourself when your mind wanders, you are strengthening your self-compassion for challenging moments in the rest of your daily life instead of criticizing yourself. You become more resilient to stress and cultivate a kinder mind.

Each time you observe the mind, that is an opportunity for 'insight' into your mind's habits and patterns; you have grown in what we might call wisdom or self-awareness.

❖ KEY FOUR: HELPFUL QUESTIONS FOR UNHELPFUL THOUGHTS

Some kinds of negative thinking patterns can be quite sticky.' You may find that you try to name it to tame it' and come back to your senses, but the thoughts continue to have a grip on you. If you find yourself in this position, you can use some further tools to untangle your thoughts and change your focus. These are called helpful questions for unhelpful thoughts. These are drawn from ACT (acceptance and commitment therapy).

You can use some of these questions to mentally question negative thoughts and use others to change your focus.

Here are some questions you can ask yourself to help you untangle from the thought. You ask them, and then you can answer them in your head. Usually, you would just pick one of these at any given time.

- Is this thought in any way useful or helpful?
- Is it true? (Can I know that it's true)
- Is this just an old story that my mind is playing out of habit?

- Does this thought help me take effective action?
- Is this thought helpful, or is my mind just babbling on?

Then you can (mentally) ask these questions below to create a new focus and new possibilities. These questions will help you focus on constructive thoughts and actions and help you effectively face your day-to-day challenges and move towards living a more meaningful life. Again, you may only use of of these at a time, but you could always try more than one too.

- What is the truth? My deepest truth?
- What do I really want to feel or create in the situation? How can I move towards that?
- How can I make the best of this situation?
- Who would I be without this negative thought?
- What new story or thought can I focus on now?
- How can I see this in a different or new way?
- What can I be grateful for at this moment?

With these powerful questions, you can change your focus from being stuck in negativity to being focused on what's going well. They will also help you take constructive action and move towards living a more meaningful life.

Constructive thinking allows you to be happy when things are going well and puts problems in perspective when times get tough so you can stay calm and clear-headed and deal with them in a practical, efficient way.

## PRACTICING THE FOUR KEYS

As mentioned above, the four keys are not a 'quick fix' method for creating permanent change of long-standing patterns. True change takes time, but I promise you with a bit of patience and practice, these four keys have the capacity to truly change your world from the inside out.

Now at the same time as I say, these are not a quick, permanent fix; you will find that in any given moment of negativity, these tools (especially 'name it to tame it' and the helpful questions) can assist you to immediately untangle and change your mindset.

The more you practice these tools, the more they will become second nature to you. It's like building a muscle—the more you use them, you become mentally fitter and stronger. In time the old habits are worn away, and rather than being preoccupied with negativity, you'll become more calm, centered, and self-aware, leading to better relationships, greater overall happiness, and a sense that your life is being fully lived.

As time goes on, you'll become more and more like those ocean depths, less affected by the ripples on the surface and more connected to the peace and wholeness at the heart of who you are.

## Short Breathing Exercise On How To Overcome Negativity

❖ Mindful Breathing

This type of exercise doesn't involve breath manipulation—it's just about placing awareness on its natural occurrence. Sounds simple, but it's not always easy to do. Begin by breathing normally and becoming a focused observer of your breath. It's helpful to hone in on a physical cue, like the rise and fall of your belly or the sensation of air in your nostrils (cool air coming in, warmer air going out). When your mind naturally wanders (and it will—that's inevitable), make a note of it, then simply return to the occurrence of each inhale and exhale.

Breathing in this way, even for a minute or two, helps eliminate distraction, release negative thoughts, improve self-awareness, and quiet a racing mind. The more you do it, the easier it will get

—and the more you'll start to notice the benefits in your daily life.

❖   Counting Breaths

Here's a similar mindful breathing technique that incorporates another mental cue to help you concentrate: counting each breath. You'll notice that it's surprisingly hard to follow your breath—one good trick for staying on task is to count it.

"For people who have really busy minds, adding the component of counting is very helpful," Price says. "Techniques like counting help take us out of thought loops that feed stress, anxiety, or negative emotions."

❖   Deep Breathing

Here, you can start to practice changing your breath—deepening it—for the desired outcome. Deep breathing, also called belly breathing or diaphragmatic breathing, is exactly what it sounds like and can help reduce stress and promote a sense of calm. Breathing very fully into the belly, then exhaling completely, works to deactivate the stress response and activate the "rest and digest" state.

Stressed? Overwhelmed? Panicked? Spend a few intentional minutes taking calm, deep (but gentle) breaths, which will signal to your brain that everything is OK.

❖   2-4 Breathing

This type of breathwork involves extending the exhale, so it's longer than the inhale. Emphasizing the exhale is meant to stimulate the parasympathetic nervous system (PNS), the calming counterpart to our stress-induced sympathetic nervous system (SNS). While the SNS accelerates heartbeat, breathing, and blood flow, the PNS slows breathing, heart rate, blood pressure, and metabolism. When your stress response is in overdrive (and whose isn't?), promote serious relaxation with a 2-4 breathing exercise: inhale for two counts and immediately exhale for four counts.

❖   Energizing Breaths

You can harness the breath to perk yourself up, too. "When you're feeling sluggish, invigorate your mind and boost energy and alertness with this breathing technique, based on a Kundalini yoga technique called segmented breathing," Price says. Inhale in four equal but distinct segments to fill the lungs, then exhale in one long, smooth segment to empty the lungs completely (repeat three or four times).

# WHY YOU ARE NOT YOUR THOUGHT

*"You are not your thoughts; you are the observer of your thoughts."—Amit Ray.*

Our inner experience is largely composed of thoughts. We create and listen to a running narrative of our life. We think about the past. We think about the future. We react. We judge. We wonder. We ponder. We remember. We plan. We predict.

It's easy to get wrapped up in all that thinking and mistakenly believe it's who we really are. But we are not our thoughts. Perhaps our thoughts are part of who we are, along with our feelings, our inclinations, and our personality. But the self is surely something greater than the sum of its parts.

**So, if you're not your thoughts, who are you?**

One answer is that you are the observer of your thoughts. You are the entity that listens to your thoughts. Another answer is that you are the director of your thoughts. This feels better because it puts you in the driver's seat. However, your thoughts frequently arise automatically without any direction from you at all. Sometimes you get to be the director, but often you are just the observer.

You are also the observer of your emotions and the director of your actions. But again, you are more than the sum of your parts. You are also not your feelings, so emotions like jealousy and rage don't make you a bad person. And you are not your actions, so making a mistake doesn't mean you're an idiot, and doing something selfish doesn't mean you're immoral.

Maybe one day, psychologists and neuroscientists will solve the riddle of consciousness. Maybe one day we'll have a better answer to this question. For now, you can rest assured that you are not your thoughts.

## Automatic Thoughts

Your automatic thoughts are a product of human nature interacting with your current environment along with all your past experiences, your upbringing, your culture, and your beliefs. Your thoughts tend to reflect your current feelings, and your feelings change pretty often. Your thoughts are often simple, short-sighted reactions to events and situations. But you are a complicated, dynamic person with long-term goals, You are not your thoughts.

We all have thoughts we're not proud of. And we often feel ashamed of ourselves for having those thoughts because we mistakenly believe they are a reflection of our true selves. But the very fact that we don't like those thoughts means we're not those thoughts. We are the observer of those thoughts. We are the entity noticing that those thoughts don't fit with who we want to be.

If you have a thought that doesn't align with your values, you can choose to reject that thought. You can argue against it and assert yourself. You can replace it with a better thought. You can work to cultivate helpful mindsets in order to improve the character of your habitual thoughts.

Likewise, if your thoughts encourage you to behave like someone you don't want to be, you can choose to behave in other ways. Your behavior is a stronger reflection of who you really are because your behavior is easier for you to control and because actions speak louder than thoughts. So try to make sure your automatic thoughts don't immediately trigger regrettable behaviors. Take time to pause and deliberately choose your actions.

## Becoming a Better Observer

Through practice, you can increasingly become a better observer of your thoughts. Doing so will make you a more powerful director of your thoughts, giving you, the real you, greater control over both your inner experience and your behavior.

Here's an example. When someone is rude to you, you might have a thought like, He's such a jerk! Instead of simply believing it, you can notice the thought for what it is and then say to yourself; I'm having the thought that he's a jerk. Doing this allows you to take a step back from your thought, which gives you an opportunity to consider it dispassionately. Maybe he didn't mean to be rude. Maybe he's been having a very difficult week, and he's not normally like this. Maybe you're sometimes like that yourself. Or maybe he really is a jerk.

If you don't notice that your thoughts are thoughts, then you'll probably just believe them and then embody them with your emotions and your behaviors, so it's important to deliberately practice being a conscious observer of your thoughts. Mindfulness meditation is an excellent way to do that, which is why one of the key benefits of mindfulness is increased free will.

The point here is that when you allow yourself to be your thoughts, you lose much of your agency over how you respond to life. If you want to approach life proactively, and I hope you do, then you'll need to remember that you are not your thoughts.

Knowing that you are not your thoughts puts that space between the stimulus and your response.

The next time you run into a disturbing thought or emotion, re-member that it does not define or control you. You can actively choose whether to participate in it or not.

It may not seem like it at the moment; thoughts and feelings are always fleeting. When you wake up in the morning, you may feel as if you are going to be tired the rest of the day but, if you just get out of bed, you can be wide awake and alert within minutes.

All thoughts and feelings are like clouds in the sky. They arrive, float around for a while, and then dissipate. It's up to you to choose if you want to get entangled in them or let them go.

You could make the argument that we spend more time thinking than doing anything else, and you'd probably be right.

But despite all this time we spend thinking—the average person has over 50,000 thoughts a day[1]—how often do we question or examine the way we relate to our thoughts?

For example,

- where do your thoughts come from?

- Do you believe everything that pops into your head?

- Do your thoughts represent who you are as a person?

- Are you the voice behind your thoughts?

We're conditioned to believe that we are the voice behind our thoughts.

At first glance, this seems to make sense. After all, is there anything more personal than our thoughts? Thoughts obviously occur in our minds alone, and we are the only ones who will ever experience them. So what could represent our "true self" more than the internal dialogue that seemingly narrates and interprets every moment of our life experience?

To answer this question, we must first ask: where do thoughts come from?

There are two major perspectives on where thoughts come from. I'm sure there are more formal names for each, but for the purposes of this article, let's call them the self-created theory and the mind-created theory.

## THE SELF-CREATED THEORY OF THOUGHT

The "self-created" theory argues that you are the voice behind your thoughts. According to the self-created theory, your thoughts are a direct extension of your identity—your character, personality, and true desires.

Every thought supposedly happens for a reason because your identity is connected to everything you think—so if you were to have what some religions consider to be "impure" thoughts, you would be considered an impure person or a sinner by those guidelines.

"Self-created" is the way most of us grow up relating to our thoughts, especially if we were raised in religious households. People who subscribe to this theory are particularly vulnerable to feelings of shame and inadequacy because they feel personally responsible for the content of each and every thought that arises, even those that contradict their deepest moral convictions.

The self-created theory also argues that there is no randomness in the thoughts you experience — if you have grotesque thoughts, then there is supposedly something grotesque with you and your true character, beliefs, and desires. In other words, every thought is an agent on your behalf.

If you believe that thoughts are self-created, you might find yourself occasionally reacting to negative thoughts with questions and statements like these:

- "Is that who I really am?"
- "Is that what I truly believe?

"Only a sick person would think something like that."

"I've thought it so many times that it must be true or have some significance."

Among other things, the main problem with the self-created theory is that you assume responsibility for thoughts you don't actually produce (more on that in a second). The self-created theory also gives negative thoughts more attention than they deserve — thoughts carry infinite shock value when you assume they stem from the core of your self.

If you believe in the self-created theory, a particularly shocking thought might tempt you to scrounge up evidence to prove it wrong and distance it from your character. You might recoil at the thoughts circling around in your brain and feel both responsible and ashamed for their contents, even though the majority of what you experience is extremely common — similar if not identical flavors of thought are experienced by both your peers and the billions that came before you.

Eventually, if you become repulsed enough by your thoughts, you might begin to question your sanity. "Am I the only one who thinks this way? What if my friends could live a day in my brain?"

Of course, the self-created theory is an exhausting and terrifying way to think because you can constantly be ambushed by your own mind and deduce shameful misunderstandings about your own character.

It's important to note that, by default, most of us come to believe we're the voice behind our thoughts, though this is often less of choice and more a coming-to-age misunderstanding about the nature of how things are — "thoughts occur in my mind, therefore I created them and they are extensions of my identity."

It's an easy and understandable assumption to make, but it's also fatal. As long as you assume responsibility for the creation of your thoughts, your well-being is at risk.

**THE MIND-CREATED THEORY OF THOUGHT**

The second theory is that thoughts are "mind-created"—instead of being the creator of your thoughts, you are a witness to them as they occur. According to the mind-created theory, thoughts are random, involuntary suggestions more-so than actual definitive truths, less symbolic of "you" and your identity in particular and more representative of the tendencies, workings, and reactions of the human mind.

Just as the main function of the respiratory system is to help you breathe, the mind's main function is to produce thought. Thoughts are not personal. Even though you experience a thought-monologue nearly all the time, thoughts aren't byproducts of your character or true self.

*As Alan Watts put it, "The mind grows thoughts as the field grows grass." Thoughts are just what the mind does.*

If you've lived your whole life thinking of yourself to be the voice behind your thoughts, you probably won't agree with the mind-created theory. You might argue that you feel as though you're controlling your thoughts and have been for your entire life. Maybe it seems even seem cold and deterministic to just consider the notion that you aren't in control of what you think.

## ARE YOUR THOUGHTS TRUE?

Obviously, the origin of thought is not as black-and-white as the presentation of these two theories might suggest.

But the main question these theories are trying to answer is — which has a greater influence on the thoughts we experience — the mind or the self?

Another way of looking at it: the self-created theory argues that the mind is contained within the self, while the mind-created theory argues that the self is contained within the mind.

If thoughts originate firmly within the self, then they might best be taken literally, seriously, and factually. But if thoughts are simply another byproduct of the mind—an external agent separate from the self—then they lose a sense of authority, urgency, and permanence. They lose the fascist ability to fully dictate what we think of ourselves and the world around us.

## YOU ARE NOT YOUR THOUGHTS

"You are not the one who speaks your thoughts, you are the one that hears them."

When we believe that we are the source of our thoughts, when our identity is mixed into everything we think, we suffer. We're suddenly prone to overly emotional reactions and take everything exponentially more seriously.

Because we can't control what we think, the self-created theory puts our quality of life at the mercy of an unreliable driver, and we spend more time lost in the fray of our minds than in reality.

But when we acknowledge that thoughts randomly emerge into our consciousness—and that we did not create the thoughts we experience—we free ourselves from their burden.

Suddenly we don't have to "catch" thoughts, interrogate them, try to trace back how they relate to our identity, or feel ashamed for their contents. We don't have to exhaustingly engage with every thought that arises. They are not ours to catch. We can simply acknowledge their presence and let them fall to the floor or drift away untouched.

If you strongly identify with your thoughts, as most do, the mind-created theory might leave a big gap in your identity. If you aren't the source of your thoughts, then what are you?

This perspective of the observer is liberating because you don't absorb the responsibility for determining whether or not a certain thought is true, whether it's really what you think or what it might say about your character. A thought does not become "yours" simply because it occurred in your mind.

Instead of getting up caught up in the storm, you can see the waves for what they are: just another natural cycle repeating itself, over and over again, as it has for millions of years. This time is no different, and it's not an emergency. It's just what the mind does.

# TRAINING YOUR MIND

**Happiness is not the endless pursuit of pleasant experiences - that sounds more like a recipe for        exhaustion - but a way of being that results from cultivating a benevolent mind, emotional balance, inner freedom, inner peace, and wisdom. Each of these qualities is a skill that can be enhanced through training the mind. -**

**Matthieu Ricard**

**Your brain is built to reinforce and regulate your life.**

Your subconscious mind has something called a homeostatic impulse, which regulates functions like body temperature, heartbeat, and breathing. Brian Tracy explained it like this: "Through your autonomic nervous system, [your homeostatic impulse] maintains a balance among the hundreds of chemicals in your billions of cells so that your entire physical machine functions in complete harmony most of the time."

But what many people don't realize is that just as your brain is built to regulate your physical self, as does it try to regulate your mental self. Your mind is constantly filtering and bringing to your attention information and stimuli that affirm your preexisting beliefs (this is known in psychology as confirmation bias), as well as presenting you with repeated thoughts and impulses that mimic and mirror that which you've done in the past.

Your subconscious mind is the gatekeeper of your comfort zone.

It is also the realm in which you can either habituate yourself to expect and routinely seek the actions that would build and reinforce the greatest success, happiness, wholeness, or healing of your life.

## The mind is a metaphor.

If an image is worth a thousand words, a metaphor is worth a thousand images. Especially to explain the concept of 'mind.'

Technology provides a helpful analogy: the brain is the hardware; the mind is the software. The first is more tangible, the latter more abstract. One has the capacity and power that can be augmented; the other can be programmed.

This approach has as many supporters as detractors. It sparks a never-ending debate.

Like any science, psychology depends on making links from the known to the unknown. Throughout the history of psychology, metaphors have proved an invaluable way of gaining purchase on the unobservables of human cognition. Indeed, a history of metaphors of mind might look very much like a history of psychology. I look at how psychologists' mind-metaphors overlap with and diverge from those used by other writers and ask what we might gain from a closer examination of the metaphors that guide us.

❖ How to train your mind: the ACT triangle

The brain is of the thinking realm; the mind is of the witnessing realm.

We are a brain-centered society. That's why people have a hard time observing their thoughts. I've been accused of discouraging people from thinking simply because I said that our thoughts cause most of our problems.

To overcome your issues, sometimes, you need to observe your thoughts rather than continue thinking.

**Give your brain a break**.

That's the power of mindfulness. As it's a sense of presence and accuracy in terms of being here. We can only operate on one dot-at-a-time — mindfulness is approaching our life that same way.

*The Buddhist Psychologist defines Mindfulness as "being watchful rather than watching something."*

**Mindfulness is personal; it's your experience**.

ACT — Acceptance Commitment Therapy — defines Psychological Flexibility as the ability to be in the present moment with full awareness and openness to our experience and to take action guided by our values.

ACT triangle image open up be present and do what matters

Open up: Both Defusion and acceptance are about separating from our thoughts and emotions — seeing them for what they are, making room for them, without judging.

**Be Present:** It's about contacting with the here-and-now, involving both verbal and non-verbal aspects of your experience — observing our own self from a different place.

**Do What Matters**: Your values should guide your goals — commit to living a life based on what matters to you.

This triangle is an effective way to train your mind. Though it's a continuum, it helps identifies the areas that you want to exercise the most.

Open your mind

*"Happiness can be achieved through training the mind." — Dalai Lama.*

Acceptance is allowing your thoughts and feelings to be as they are.

It doesn't matter if they are painful or pleasant — stop fighting reality. Let your thoughts and emotions come and go naturally without neither forcing nor silencing them.

Acceptance doesn't mean giving up. On the contrary, it's acknowledging your feelings and life events. When you accept all your experiences — both pleasant and painful — you are expanding your mind.

The opposite of acceptance is avoidance.

Painful experiences are like a wild river; we need to cross them if we want to get to the other side.

Defusion is a powerful technique to observe your thoughts rather than see through them. Your thoughts are a lens that clouds your vision. Defusion neutralizes it.

Your thoughts are wild wolves that live inside you — if you don't domesticate them, they will eat you alive. Defusion brings clarity — it's about separating yourself from your thoughts rather than getting stuck in them. Taming the inner wolves requires stopping living on autopilot.

Mindfulness is not a distraction technique; it is not meant for you to avoid your thoughts. If negative feelings come up, notice them, and move on.

Simply label your thoughts as "thoughts" without reacting or judging them. You can make fun of your thoughts or turn them into objects. There are many defusion exercises that can help tame your mind.

Remember, mindfulness is the opposite of living on autopilot.

## Train your Observing Self

Being present requires focus. To pay attention to what's happening here and now. To stop thinking about the past or speculating about the future. Bring your awareness to this instant.

That's easier said than done, though.

Elevators are a perfect example of how hard it is to be present. What do we usually do? We get anxious because we can't face not having anything to do. Instead of being present, we look at our phone screens. We avoid paying attention to what's going on.

The past we cannot change. We cannot control the future either. Being present is connecting to your nowness. The more you are in touch with your feelings, the more you can regulate your behaviors.

When you are lost in your thoughts, you are missing out on life in the present.

The Thinking-Self and the Observing-Self are the two significant aspects of your mind.

The Observing-Self is not a thought or a feeling but more an awareness — it's a perspective from which you observe your experiences from the distance.

Your thoughts are constantly changing: at times, they can be joyful, painful, or pleasant. The same is true for your feelings: sometimes you feel anxious, sad, upset, or frustrated.

The Observing-Self is the part of you that does not change but experiences — it neither judges nor takes any responsibility. Whereas the Thinking-Self is the part of you that judges, the Observing Self helps you to become aware of what you are doing.

The Observing-Self is like the sky. Your thoughts and emotions are like the weather. No matter how strong the storms, they can't damage the sky. It always has room for more — sooner or later, the weather will change for the better.

This simple exercise will help you practice being present.

You can practice this exercise at your next meeting to gain focus. Or try it next time you catch an elevator; you'll realize everything you are missing when you are living on autopilot.

## Train your mind for action

Who or what will you serve?

Your values determine what you serve in life.

We are a goal driven-society. That's dangerous: your goals shouldn't determine your values but the other way around. Your goals are in the future; your values are in the present.

Values are not emotions. They are directions, not outcomes. They help you define what to say 'yes' to and, most importantly, what you say 'no' to. Your values shape your priorities.

Acceptance is the first step. However, life is more than merely overcoming your emotions and thoughts. To achieve fulfillment, you must live a life according to your values.

## What's your life's purpose?

Clarity helps you move into action. When you know the kind of life you want to live, when you know the impact you want to create, when you know what matters to you, it's easier to make things happen.

However, clarity is not rigid but fluid. Storms can cloud what you see, but the sky is still there. Be patient. When you feel lost, treat yourself kindly. Once the storm passes, you will be able to see what matters to you again.

## Move from FEAR to DARE

"First say to yourself what you would be, and then do what you have to do." — Epictetus.

Training your mind requires moving from avoidance to acceptance. To overcome your fears and be courageous to live the life you want.

FEAR is an acronym for Fusion (seeing through your thoughts), Excessive goals (unrealistic or unclear), Avoidance of discomfort (blaming things into others and living in denial), and Remoteness from values (lack of clarity or alignment between what matters to you and what you do).

**DARE is the antidote to FEAR.**

Defusion: You can acknowledge your thoughts and emotions. You don't let them cloud your vision. You see them but don't see life through them.

- Acceptance of discomfort: Life is not easy. Only those who can make room for unpleasant experiences and feelings can overcome them. Being in denial won't make your problems disappear.

- Realistic goals: Do you have the skills needed to achieve your goals? Can you get them, or should you adjust your goals to your current abilities? Being realistic is not lowering your bar but avoiding unnecessary frustrations. Sometimes setting micro-goals is smarter. The more you achieve, the more you can achieve.

- Embracing Values: Are your actions aligned with your values? This is one of the most common reasons why people get stuck. Lack of motivation is typically correlated to a lack of clarity or doing things that don't matter to oneself.

These acronyms — from Act make simple — are not a formula but a framework. Use them as a self-reflection tool to understand and overcome barriers.

Your mind is your most valuable asset; training not only takes a lifetime — it's the most critical priority in your life.

❖   13 Ways To Start Training Your Subconscious Mind To Get What You Want

**Your brain is built to reinforce and regulate your life.**

Your subconscious mind has something called a homeostatic impulse, which regulates functions like body temperature, heartbeat, and breathing. Brian Tracy explained it like this: "Through your autonomic nervous system, [your homeostatic impulse] maintains a balance among the hundreds of chemicals in your billions of cells so that your entire physical machine functions in complete harmony most of the time."

But what many people don't realize is that just as your brain is built to regulate your physical self, as does it try to regulate your mental self. Your mind is constantly filtering and bringing to your attention information and stimuli that affirm your pre-existing beliefs (this is known in psychology as confirmation bias), as well as presenting you with repeated thoughts and impulses that mimic and mirror that which you've done in the past.

**Your subconscious mind is the gatekeeper of your comfort zone.**

It is also the realm in which you can either habituate yourself to expect and routinely seek the actions that would build and reinforce the greatest success, happiness, wholeness, or healing of your life.

Here, a few ways to start retraining your mind to be your ally, not your enemy.

1. Be willing to see the unchangeable change.

The first step in creating massive change in your life is not actually believing that it's possible; it's willing to see if it is possible.

You are not going to be able to jump from being a complete skeptic to a wholehearted believer. The step between those is just being open to seeing what could be possible. You could maybe try sending a few "scary emails," in which you propose a client or partner for something that they do not have any reason to respond to. You might have a few dozen ignored messages, but eventually, someone will respond.

The point is that you're willing to see if it's possible... that's what will change your life.

2. Give yourself permission to be successful.

Instead of regurgitating the same old narrative of believing you'll be happy once you're 10 pounds, one promotion, and two life events down-the-line, work on changing your inner monologue to: "I allow my life to be good."

Give yourself permission to be happy and successful and not feel guilty about it. If you have a subconscious association between success being amoral or corrupt, of course, you're not going to do what you need to do to live the life you want to live. Instead, give yourself permission to step into a whole, happy, healthy, grounded, and meaningful existence.

3. Don't allow other people's fears to cast shadows of doubt.

The way people respond to news of your success will tell you how they are really doing in their lives.

If you announce your engagement, people who are in happy marriages will be elated for you. People who are in unhappy marriages will warn you that it is difficult and that you should enjoy your remaining time as "single" individuals.

The point is that other people's fears are projections of their own situations. They have nothing to do with what you are or aren't capable of.

4. Surround yourself with positive reinforcement.

Keep a bottle of champagne in the fridge. Change your morning alarm on your phone to read the message: "CONGRATULA-TIONS!!!" Make sure that the items that you see and touch most often bring you positivity and hopefulness. Keep an inspirational note on a post-it next to your computer. Unfollow people who make you feel bad about yourself and follow those who are constantly posting motivational messages and interesting ideas. Make your newsfeed a place that can catalyze your growth instead of lessening your perception of your worth.

5. Speak your success as a present fact, not a future plan.

Though you shouldn't say things like "I drive a convertible," or "I am a CEO," if they are not, in fact, true, do start speaking about what it is you want out of life, not in the context that you will one day pursue it, but that you are already living it.

Instead of saying: "I hope to do that one day," say, "I am strategizing how to do that now." Instead of thinking: "I will be happy when I am in a different place in my life," think, "I am completely capable of being happy right here and right now, nothing is holding me back."

6. Create a visual space.

Being able to imagine what it is you want out of your life is absolutely essential for creating it because if you don't know where you're going, you won't know which way to turn first.

Once you have a crystal clear image in your mind for what it is you want and how it is you want to live, you are then capable of beginning to enact and create it. If you are still hazy or torn between what you want, you will be rendered incapable of taking real, meaningful action toward anything.

Whether you use a Pinterest board, blog, notebook, or board, put together words and images that represent what you want and how you want to live.

7. Identify your resistance.

When our subconscious minds hold us back from pursuing something that we love, it is because we are holding a conflicting belief about it.

To identify your resistance, question yourself. Ask yourself why you feel better when you procrastinate or why getting what you really want could actually put you in a place that makes you feel more vulnerable than ever. Find a way to meet those needs before you proceed.

8. Have a master plan for your life.

Forget five or even ten-year plans; so many changes over time it's nearly impossible to set goals that you'll be able to keep. Most likely, new or even better opportunities will surface, and though your life won't look like you thought it would, you're better off for that.

Instead, have a master plan. Identify your core values and motivations. Ask yourself what the ultimate goal of what you want to accomplish while you are alive is; imagine the kind of legacy you want to leave. Once you have your Big Picture values identified, you can make decisions for the long-term that align with your true self.

9. Start a gratitude journal.

The best way to start putting yourself in a headspace of "having" rather than "wanting" is to begin a gratitude practice. By expressing thanks for all that you do have, you shift your mindset from being hungry for change to feeling satisfied with where you are at. Nothing magnetizes abundance to you like gratitude. There's a saying that once you believe you have enough, you are open to receiving more and more and more. That is undoubtedly true.

10. Start asking for what you want, even if you know you'll be denied.

If someone asks you to do a consulting project, ask for the amount of money you truly want to earn for it. If your goal is to get a promotion in your organization, sit down with your higher up and make your intentions known. Reach out to brands you want to work with. Start asking for what you want, even if you have no reason to believe that anyone will actually give you any of those things. Eventually, they will.

11. Release your attachment to the "how."

Your job is to identify the what and then to work in tandem with other people for the how.

If your goal is to work remotely and run your own business, instead of giving up if your first attempt fails, try reimagining how else you could achieve your ultimate vision in a new way that is more financially lucrative.

The point is that life will always surprise you with how things come to fruition. Instead of being obsessively attached to every little detail working out the way you think, it should be open to potential and possibility, even if it's something you never imagined before.

12. Surround yourself with allies.

Start spending time with people who are ambitious, supportive, and creative.

If you're hanging out every weekend with people who are likewise as unhappy with their lives, you aren't going to receive an abundance of support if you try to break free and do your own thing. Remember that you will truly become who you spend the most time with, and choose who that is very carefully.

13. Fill your "dead air" time with affirmation and motivation.

When you're on your commute each morning, listen to a motivational speech or podcast. While you're doing the dishes or driving, tune into a talk show that relates to the type of business you're trying to do. Infuse your life with as much affirmation and motivation as possible. You may need to hear the lessons more than once, but they will seep into your brain over time, and eventually, you will find yourself acting on wisdom received from those who are where you want to be.

❖   Seven Brain Exercises to Strengthen Your Mind

While you might know that you need to exercise your body, did you know that it might also be important to exercise your mind? You've probably heard the old adage "use it or lose it." Many do believe that this maxim applies to your brain health.

Brain training is all the rage these days, often touted as a way to sharpen your mind and even boost intelligence. While many cognitive scientists suggest that the claims surrounding brain training are both exaggerated and misleading, there is an abundance of research suggesting that certain types of activities can be beneficial for your brain's health.

**Take Care of Your Body to Take Care of Your Mind**

If you want to take care of your mind, you need to start by taking care of your body.

Research has time and time again shown that people who engage in healthy behaviors such as exercise and proper nutrition are less susceptible to the cognitive declines associated with the aging process.

We definately found that men who practiced certain healthy behaviors were around 60% less likely to experience cognitive impairment and dementia as they age.

These healthy behaviors included not smoking, maintaining a healthy, regularly exercising, consuming lots of vegetables and fruits, and consuming a low to moderate alcohol amount.

So if you want to build a better mind, start by working on your physical health first. Go for a walk, start incorporating more fresh fruits and vegetables into your diet, and try to give up any bad habits like excessive alcohol consumption or tobacco use. Some of these might be more difficult than others, but your brain will thank you for years to come.

## Draw a Map of Your Town From Memory

While you might feel like you can navigate the streets of your neighborhood with your eyes closed, try challenging your brain by actually drawing a map of your town or neighborhood from memory. No cheating! Try to include major streets, major side streets, and local landmarks.

Once you are done, compare your memory map to a real map of the area. How did you do? Are you surprised by some of the things that you missed? If you found this activity too easy, try drawing a less familiar area from memory, such as a map of the entire United States or Europe, and labeling every state or country.

Navigating your way to the supermarket or doctor's office might seem simple and almost automatic when you are behind the wheel of your car. However, forcing yourself to remember the layout of your neighborhood and draw and label it helps activate a variety of areas of your brain.

## Learn Something New

This brain exercise requires a bit of commitment, but it is also one that just might give you the most bang for your buck. Learning something new is one way to keep your brain on its toes and continually introduce new challenges.

I realised that assigned older adults to learn various new skills ranging from digital photography to quilting. They then did memory tests and compared the experimental groups to control groups. Those in the control groups had engaged in a fun but not mentally challenging activities, such as watching movies and listening to the radio.

I also found that only those who had learned a new skill experienced improved memory tests.

They also discovered that these memory improvements were still present when tested again a year later.

Some things you might want to try to include learning a new language, learning to play a musical instrument, or learning a new hobby. Not only will you be stretching your mind, but you will also be continually learning something new as you keep expanding your skills and becoming more accomplished.

## Try Using Your Non-Dominant Hand

Up next is an interesting brain exercise that one neurobiologist suggests might help "keep your brain alive."

Make use of Neurobic Exercises to Help Prevent Memory Loss and Increase Mental Fitness, using your non-dominant hand to strengthen your mind. Because using your opposite hand can be so challenging, it can be a great way to increase brain activity.

Try switching hands while you are eating dinner or when you are trying to write something down. It will be difficult, but that is exactly the point.

The most effective brain activities are those that are not necessarily easy.

Up next is an activity that you probably do every day, but you might not realize just how beneficial it might be for your mental strength.

**Socialize**

Socializing tends to engage multiple areas of the brain, and many social activities also include physical elements, such as playing a sport, that are also beneficial to your mind.

Even if you are a chronic introvert, seeking social interactions can benefit your brain in both the short and long-term. Some ideas for staying socially engaged to include signing up for volunteer opportunities in your community, joining a club, signing up for a local walking group, and staying in close touch with your friends and family.

**Meditate**

Up next is a brain exercise that has been in use for thousands of years but has recently gained considerable recognition for its effectiveness.

One brain exercise you might not have considered might actually be extremely effective – meditation. Mindfulness meditation, in particular, is all the rage at the moment, Before you say that ancient meditation tradition is too New Age for you, consider some of the research demonstrating the many benefits of meditation.

Once you've tried some of these brain exercises, you might be left wondering if any of those online "brain training" websites might also help. Next up, let's explore whether or not those sites, apps, and programs might really be worth your time.

**What About All Those Brain Training Games?**

Chances are probably pretty good that you've at least heard, or even tried, some of the many brain training games, websites, and apps that are out there. Many of these tools claim that these computerized brain exercises can increase your mental flexibility, keep you mentally sharper as you age and even make you more intelligent.

While there is still plenty of debate about whether or not these claims are true, there is a chance that playing these types of mental games might is good for your brain.

How much exactly is still up for debate. If you think you would enjoy such games, you can find a nice list of brain training resources that you might want to check out.

If, however, you already spend too much time staring at your computer screen or smartphone, your time is probably much better well spent going out for a stroll, enjoying a new hobby, or even visiting with a friend. All of these activities can have major long-term effects on the health and vitality of your brain.

# STOP COMPARING YOURSELF TO OTHERS

**"Don't compare yourself to others. You have no idea what their journey is all about."- Regina Brett.**

Comparing ourselves to others allows them to drive our behavior. This type of comparison is between you and someone else. Sometimes it's about something genetic, like wishing to be taller, but more often, it's about something the other person is capable of doing that we wish we could do as well. Maybe Sally writes better reports than you, and maybe Bob has a happier relationship with his spouse than you do. Sometimes this comparison is motivating, and sometimes it's destructive.

You can be anything, but you can't be everything. When we compare ourselves to others, we're often comparing their best features against our average ones. It's like being right-handed and trying to play an instrument with your left hand. Not only do we naturally want to be better than them, the unconscious realization that we do not often become self-destructive.

Comparisons between people are a recipe for unhappiness unless you are the best in the world. Which, let's be honest, only one person is. Not only are we unhappy, but the other people are as well. They are probably comparing themselves to you—maybe you're better at networking than they are, and they're jealous. At worst, when we compare ourselves to others, we end up focusing our energy on bringing them down instead of raising ourselves up.

There is one thing that you're better at than other people: being you. This is the only game you can really win.

When you start with this mindset, the world starts to look better again. No longer are you focused on where you stand relative to others? Instead, your focus and energy are placed on what you're capable of now and how you can improve yourself.

Life becomes about being a better version of yourself. And when that happens, your effort and energy go toward upgrading your personal operating system every day, not worrying about what your coworkers are doing. You became happier, free from the shackles of false comparisons, and focused on the present moment.

When what you do doesn't meet the expectations of others, too bad. The way they look at you is the same way you were looking at them, though a distorted lens shaped by experiences and expectations. What really matters is what you think about what you do, what your standards are, what you can learn today.

That's not an excuse to ignore thoughtful opinions—other people might give you a picture of how you fall short of being your best self. Instead, it's a reminder to compare yourself to who you were this morning. Are you better than you were when you woke up? If not, you've wasted a day. It's less about others and more about how you improve relative to who you were.

When you stop comparing between people and focus internally, you start being better at what really matters: being you. It's simple but not easy.

The most important things in life are measured internally. Thinking about what matters to you is hard. Playing to someone else's scoreboard is easy; that's why a lot of people do it. But winning the wrong game is pointless and empty. You get one life. Play your own game.

## Life's Enough: Stop Comparing Yourself to Others

If you took the strengths of others and compared them to your weaknesses, how do you think you'd size up? And do you think this would make you feel good?

The funny thing is, this is what most of us do at one time or another — and some of us do pretty often.

It's a sure-fire recipe for a drop in self-confidence and for unhappiness. It's also not that useful.

## When You Focus on What You Do, You're Too Busy to Compare Yourself with Others

With social media announcing every friend's promotion, latest holiday, house purchase, engagement, or wedding, it can sometimes lead us to feel inadequate about our own lives, especially if we feel we're 'falling behind' in life.

But the comparison game is a dangerous one. The pressure to keep up with how other people are living their lives compared to our own can leave us feeling depressed and takes away the focus we have on our goals and our own unique life path.

Why Comparing Ourselves with Others Is Problematic

If comparing and measuring ourselves with others brings the

tendency to make us feel 'less-than,' why do we put ourselves through it?

According to the social comparison theory, fundamentally, we're social creatures, and we have an overwhelming need to understand ourselves and our place in the world. This includes those around us and especially our closest peers.

Social comparisons are separated into two categories – downward comparison (comparing yourself to somebody worse off than you) and upward comparison (comparing yourself with those who are perceived as better off than you). These two can both create problems with how we view ourselves.

While the downward comparison may seem like a way to make us feel better about ourselves, it actually means we're tying our confidence and self-esteem to the misfortune of others. It also causes us to focus too much on negative aspects of people rather than seeing the whole picture.

And, of course, upward comparison can allow us to feel motivated and inspired, but our negative minds tend to sway towards fuelling envy or unrealistic standards. This means we overlook the complexity of our own lives and focus on the 'highlight reel' of somebody else's.

**Most of the Time, People Don't Really Care; They're Just Curious.**

The other problem with comparison is that, although we may not have the habit of comparing ourselves, others can have the tendency to point out how we're doing compared with others.

Whether it's making a choice to not get married or have kids, or what career path we've chosen to follow (or not follow), there will likely be someone who has an opposing opinion and perspective on it. This can potentially lead us to self-doubt and even contemplating changing our decisions.

But we have to understand the importance of focusing on ourselves because others' perspectives are limited and based on their own opinions and experiences. Much of the time, it can be pure curiosity rather than having true intentions to guide us. This is why it's paramount to tune out these unneeded opinions and just focus on what you want your life to look like.

## How to Block Out Distracting Noise and Focus on Yourself

If scrolling through social media leaves you feeling down, insecure, and inadequate, or you just want to stop caring about the 'helpful' opinions others like to force on you about your life, then there are ways to shift your perspective and lead a much happier life in the process.

## Create a Clear Roadmap of Your Life

In order to be more confident in your decisions and therefore be strong enough to dismiss what others say, creating a roadmap of where you want to go and how you're going to get there will bring more stability and less insecurity. By doing this, you will care much less about what other people are doing in comparison or what they think about you.

Create a list of goals, note where you are now in relation to them (with no negative judgment), and write out an action plan for how you can achieve them. You can make a one-week plan or a one-year plan – whatever you feel comfortable with on any subject – and you'll start to feel a sense of moving forward.

## Do Some 'All-Round' Self-Improvement

Self-improvement is a wonderful way to focus on ourselves, but often we tend to self-improve when the chips are down in certain areas of our lives. For example, if we want to improve our health, we may start to eat better and exercise more.

However, it can lead us to ignore other areas such as work, learning, or relationships. Focusing on more than one area will create a feeling that we're establishing abundance overall, which, in turn, will stop us from feeling lack and causing us to compare one area of our life to someone else's.

Write out a list of how you can improve each area of your life – perhaps learning something new for a dream job, an exercise routine to get healthy, or improving your social skills in order to make new friends. Do a little bit at a time for each area, and you'll soon grow more and more confident in yourself and where your life is heading.

**Remember That Everything Takes Time**

We're often made to think that certain life goals must happen by a certain time, but it doesn't always work out that way (this is when the comparison game can be at its strongest!) Try not to focus on specific time-frames and understand that you're always on your path to where you want to go.

People go along their own path at different speeds, and that's okay. Make peace with where you are, find all you can to appreciate your life no matter how small your successes, and believe that you will achieve your goals and dreams in your own timing – timing that's best for you and no one else.

**How to Stop Comparing Yourself to Others & Celebrate Your Uniqueness**

It's easy to say but hard to follow. Most of us compare ourselves to others even though we know better.

We compare ourselves for (unknown) human reasons, as it's definitely not because it makes us better, more productive, or smarter in any way. If you simplify it, one could say that comparison is a reaction and/or an emotion.

We can't always control our emotions, but we do have the ability to control what we do with this emotion: will you let it control you, or will you take back control?

Seven steps that will help you celebrate your own unique superpowers and make you stop comparing yourself to others

## 1. Focus on Your Strengths

Like with most things, learning how to stop comparing yourself starts with a cliché. Yes, it probably feels like repetition. We all know that we should focus on our strengths and not compare ourselves to others, so why do people keep bringing it up then?

Well, most clichés are clichés for a reason. It's one of those things that people know but still somehow fail to actually take in and live by.

People have different strengths and weaknesses. You might have heard the saying:

> *A flower does not think of competing with the flower next to it. It just blooms.*

And it's true. We are all special in our unique way. Maybe we're not all born to be Winston Churchill or Albert Einstein, actually forget about then maybe – we're not all born to be Winston

Churchill or Albert Einstein. But we still have something that sets us apart from others. Sometimes in a big way, sometimes in a small way.

The problem is that we will never be able to see that if we're focused on others. When you start comparing (and competing) against others, you're most likely comparing yourself to their strengths even though the same thing might be your weakness – and how is that fair?

Turn your head to the mirror. Here's who you should compare yourself to. Find your strengths and work on them.

## 2. Awareness

It's important to be aware and realize you don't always see the full story. When we compare ourselves to others, we only see what they choose to put out there. They represent themselves in a certain way to the world on the job, on social media, and yes, basically everywhere.

As mentioned above, it will typically lead you to compare the worst of yourself to the best of others.

If you're not too sure about this statement, then take a minute to think about what you put out there for the world to see. It's not about faking it, but most people definitely filter their life. They choose very carefully what glimpses of their life they show as well as what they hideaway.

Most people probably don't know about your struggles, so how can you know anything about the person's struggles that you've been comparing yourself to?

"We live in a world where everyone is sharing one perfect second of their imperfect day, and we're interpreting that perfect second as a life of perfection. However, the reality is much different. They are living a life of quiet desperation like the rest of us".

When we compare ourselves to someone else's success, we only see the results – not the effort. You can't compare your beginnings to their ends. You might only have been on this road for a few months – and they've been on it for years.

## 3. Don't Knock Others Down

When kids and teenagers feel insecure, they have a tendency to take it out on others. Don't be a kid.

All people grow up psychically, but not everyone grows up mentally. If you find yourself knocking other people down in order to feel better about yourself – stop. Someone else's failure is never going to be your win.

Some people belittle others in order to elevate themselves, but even if you do decide to go down this (wrong) road, it won't do you any good. Why form an enemy when you could form a friend?

In the end, you'll still be in the same place you were in before. So just forget about everyone else.

This is about you, but don't knock yourself down either. It's important to remember that there's a difference between pushing yourself and punishing yourself.

## 4. Accept Your Shortcomings

If you want to grow, then you need to start out by learning and accepting all parts of yourself. You wouldn't ignore a problem to solve it, would you? Most of us probably tried at one point to realize it doesn't really work that way.

Shortcomings aren't always a problem or something we necessarily need to solve. But it's impossible to grow if you don't allow yourself to take a good look in the mirror and really get to know yourself– strengths and weaknesses.

If we don't have a starting point, it's hard to be able to see how far we've come later on, and it's this kind of reminder that often will help us keep going and motivate us in the future.

At the same time, once you figure out what you aren't good at, it will be much easier to see what you actually can do well.

And sometimes, it's our weirdness that sets us aside. There is a speech that says

*"Weirdness is why we adore our friends. Weirdness is what bonds us to our colleagues. Weirdness is what sets us apart, gets us hired. Be your unapologetically weird self. In fact, being weird may even find you the ultimate happiness."*

5. Remember: It's All About Time

There is no way around it. Comparing yourself to other people is a waste of time. It's not productive in any way.

What does it really do other than taking away precious minutes (sometimes hours) from your day? We get 86.400 seconds every day. Why waste a single second on comparing yourself to others?

It won't help you. It won't make you grow in any way. It definitely won't make you feel any better.

Sometimes we don't need science or clever pep-talks. All we need is to remind ourselves of basic, which are probably true facts about life that we already know.

Take a minute to review your day and week. A little recap might help you realize how much time you've already spent on this without even knowing it. Not all wake-up calls come from your phone.

## 6. Choose Whose Input You Ingest

While it's unhealthy to compare yourself to others, it can actually be quite helpful to learn from others' habits. Habits can be adapted, and it's possible to find inspiration in others.

Take some time to fully realize who you're choosing to look up to and how it's impacting you:

What are you watching, listening to, and reading, etc.? Are you looking up to someone who's done some grown-breaking work in the field you're working in that can actually learn you something?

## 7. Learn to Love the Journey

We might just have learned something really big, had a huge win either personally or professionally, but for some reason, we're still only focused on how far away we are from our end goals.

The truth is that we will never be enough – in our own mind at least. Humans are built to keep growing. We're not supposed to reach a point where we have it all, because then what? What's the point of getting up in the morning if we already have it all?

We need a purpose. We need something new to focus on, so we're always going to want more.

Accept that you don't have to have it all to enjoy the journey. Appreciate that you have something to wake up to — a goal or something to work towards.

❖ Eight Amazing Things that Happen Once You Stop Comparing Yourself to Others

## 1. You will gain self-worth

When you compare your life to someone else's, it's usually the result of you not feeling good about yourself.

"Unfortunately, this game has few winners and leads you to the no-win trap of degrading or judging yourself or someone else. It can also lead to jealousy, anger, resentment, and even hatred for yourself or another person.

Once you let go of comparing your life to others, you allow yourself to focus on yourself and your own strengths, talents, and accomplishments. "If you're always looking at keeping up with other people or comparing yourself to other people, you're likely overlooking your own strengths and talents. You may even hide your talents and strengths,

## 2. You will clear your head

"You are essentially focused on this other person in an unhealthy manner, and wasting your precious energy on them instead of you." If you really want to have what someone else does, consider the notion that they probably worked diligently and gruelingly for what they have, and then turn that around and make it work for you by giving yourself the attention you crave and deserve

### 3.You embrace your individuality

When you compare your life to someone else's, you are setting up an unfair playing field from the start. Because no two people are exactly alike with exactly the same life experiences, it is virtually impossible to make a fair comparison between your life and someone else's. Embrace the uniqueness of what makes you who you are.

### 4.You gain self-acceptance

When you let go of caring about others' lives and their accomplishments and comparing yourself to them, you give yourself an enormous gift: the freedom to be you.

"This leads to increased self-acceptance which then boosts your self-esteem, confidence, and self-worth because you allow yourself to succeed at what you are good at,

### 5.You gain trust

When you stop comparing yourself to others, you are also increasing your trust in yourself and the universe; you gain faith that your skills and talents will be in demand and that you will come out on top. You will continue to have a brighter outlook and gain empowerment, and can focus on what you can control:

### 6. You have more gratitude

Letting go of comparisons facilitates what you should be grateful for in your own life. Write down your thoughts to stay on a healthy path. "Keeping a gratitude journal allows us to go back and reread all of the amazing things that happened in our lives and keeps us focused on the positive because we can see in black and white all of our wins.

## 7. You release a material focus

When you accept and feel grateful in your own life, you gain contentment, which transcends what you can buy.

"You embrace that you can be happy without the biggest house, the newest tech, the sleekest car – and you embrace your happiness depends solely on you. You embrace no external possession can make you happy,

## 8. You have a fulfilling life beyond social media

When you are in a good mental place, you put limits on your social media time and become better in the real world. "Realize social media and all  of the instant updates and notifications often drain our time, and our inner mean girl/guy thrives on the feeling of not being good enoug

**Stop Comparing Yourself to Others to Improve Self-Esteem**

Why should you stop comparing yourself to others? The main reason is that comparing yourself to others is destructive to your self-esteem. When you compare yourself to others, you might think they have it all together and believe you should be the same. You might treat life as a competition and base your worth in comparison to what other people are good at, their looks, personalities, what they have, or what they've achieved. You may be too hard on yourself for not being like others and fail to see your own unique qualities. Comparing yourself to others is destructive to your self-esteem--and you can learn to stop it.

Basing your worth on other people is disempowering. What others do is outside of your control, and you can't change that. However, you can change the way you view yourself. Learn to stop comparing yourself to others and build your self-esteem.

## How to Stop Comparing Yourself to Others

- Realize that your worth comes from inside. It's who you are as a person regardless of externals. It does not depend on what others are doing.
- Know that looks can be deceiving. Everyone has their own issues and insecurities, even though they're often well hidden. Nobody has a perfect life. You may think someone is doing well, but you don't have the full picture.
- Stop worrying about what others are doing. You can't control what others are doing. It's disempowering and a waste of energy to worry about it. Instead, focus on making your own life the best it can be.
- Forget about being right or wrong. Everyone has their own unique circumstances and strengths. What's right for one person may not be for another. Do what's right for you at the right time for you.
- Remember that there will always be someone better than you at something. That's life, no matter who you are. However, there are things you're better at, too. Realize that nobody's good at everything. Give yourself permission to try things out and to make mistakes.
- Have realistic expectations of yourself. Let go of perfectionism and be reasonable with your expectations.
- Know your own strengths and interests. Figure out what you're good at and what you like to do. If you're unsure, take the time to figure it out.
- Nurture your strengths. Do the things you're good at and enjoy.
- Focus on the positives about yourself. There are many positives about yourself, and it's a matter of seeing them. Focus on your good points. It might help to write them down or to practice gratitude.

- Embrace your individuality. Your uniqueness is what makes you special, and it's well worth embracing. You have so much value just by being yourself. Think of all the people who made a difference in this world just by being themselves.

Know that life's not a competition. When you stop competing with others, it's liberating, and it gives you the freedom to be the best person you can be. Instead of competing with others, aim for personal growth.

Find a purpose or meaning in what you do. What you're doing matters, and it's important to realize that.

Enjoy the journey. Don't be overly concerned about outcomes or achievements. Instead, give yourself permission to enjoy the present moment, learn and grow.

Your life is your own unique journey, and it doesn't matter what others are doing. Be the best person you can be and embrace your individuality. Stop comparing yourself to others and give yourself permission to be yourself to improve your self-esteem.

## STOP COMPARING YOURSELF TO OTHERS

*"Don't compare yourself to others. You have no idea what their journey is all about." - Regina Brett.*

Comparing ourselves to others allows them to drive our behavior. This type of comparison is between you and someone else. Sometimes it's about something genetic, like wishing to be taller, but more often, it's about something the other person is capable of doing that we wish we could do as well. Maybe Sally writes better reports than you, and maybe Bob has a happier relationship with his spouse than you do. Sometimes this comparison is motivating, and sometimes it's destructive.

You can be anything, but you can't be everything. When we compare ourselves to others, we're often comparing their best features against our average ones. It's like being right-handed and trying to play an instrument with your left hand. Not only do we naturally want to be better than them, the unconscious realization that we do not often become self-destructive.

Comparisons between people are a recipe for unhappiness unless you are the best in the world. Which, let's be honest, only one person is. Not only are we unhappy, but the other people are as well. They are probably comparing themselves to you—maybe you're better at networking than they are, and they're jealous. At worst, when we compare ourselves to others, we end up focusing our energy on bringing them down instead of raising ourselves up.

There is one thing that you're better at than other people: being you. This is the only game you can really win.

When you start with this mindset, the world starts to look better again. No longer are you focused on where you stand relative to others. Instead, your focus and energy are placed on what you're capable of now and how you can improve yourself.

Life becomes about being a better version of yourself. And when that happens, your effort and energy go toward upgrading your personal operating system every day, not worrying about what your coworkers are doing. You became happier, free from the shackles of false comparisons, and focused on the present moment.

When what you do doesn't meet the expectations of others, too bad. The way they look at you is the same way you were looking at them, though a distorted lens shaped by experiences and expectations. What really matters is what you think about what you do, what your standards are, what you can learn today.

That's not an excuse to ignore thoughtful opinions—other people might give you a picture of how you fall short of being your best self. Instead, it's a reminder to compare yourself to who you were this morning. Are you better than you were when you woke up? If not, you've wasted a day. It's less about others and more about how you improve relative to who you were.

When you stop comparing between people and focus internally, you start being better at what really matters: being you. It's simple but not easy.

The most important things in life are measured internally. Thinking about what matters to you is hard. Playing to someone else's scoreboard is easy; that's why a lot of people do it. But winning the wrong game is pointless and empty. You get one life. Play your own game.

**Life is Enough: Stop Comparing Yourself to Others**

If you took the strengths of others and compared them to your weaknesses, how do you think you'd size up? And do you think this would make you feel good?

The funny thing is, this is what most of us do at one time or another — and some of us do pretty often.

It's a sure-fire recipe for a drop in self-confidence and for unhappiness. It's also not that useful.

When You Focus on What You Do, You're Too Busy to Compare

Yourself with Others

With social media announcing every friend's promotion, latest holiday, house purchase, engagement, or wedding, it can sometimes lead us to feel inadequate about our own lives, especially if we feel we're 'falling behind' in life.

But the comparison game is a dangerous one. The pressure to keep up with how other people are living their lives compared to our own can leave us feeling depressed and takes away the focus we have on our goals and our own unique life path.

## Why Comparing Ourselves with Others Is Problematic

If comparing and measuring ourselves with others brings the tendency to make us feel 'less-than,' why do we put ourselves through it?

According to the social comparison theory, fundamentally, we're social creatures, and we have an overwhelming need to understand ourselves and our place in the world. This includes those around us and especially our closest peers.

Social comparisons are separated into two categories – downward comparison (comparing yourself to somebody worse off than you) and upward comparison (comparing yourself with those who are perceived as better off than you). These two can both create problems with how we view ourselves.

While the downward comparison may seem like a way to make us feel better about ourselves, it actually means we're tying our confidence and self-esteem to the misfortune of others. It also causes us to focus too much on negative aspects of people rather than seeing the whole picture.

And, of course, upward comparison can allow us to feel motivated and inspired, but our negative minds tend to sway towards fuelling envy or unrealistic standards. This means we overlook the complexity of our own lives and focus on the 'highlight reel' of somebody else's.

Most of the Time, People Don't Really Care; They're Just Curious.

The other problem with comparison is that, although we may not have the habit of comparing ourselves, others can have the tendency to point out how we're doing compared with others.

Whether it's making a choice to not get married or have kids, or what career path we've chosen to follow (or not follow), there will likely be someone who has an opposing opinion and perspective on it. This can potentially lead us to self-doubt and even contemplating changing our decisions.

But we have to understand the importance of focusing on ourselves because others' perspectives are limited and based on their own opinions and experiences. Much of the time, it can be pure curiosity rather than having true intentions to guide us. This is why it's paramount to tune out these unneeded opinions and just focus on what you want your life to look like.

### How to Block Out Distracting Noise and Focus on Yourself

If scrolling through social media leaves you feeling down, insecure, and inadequate, or you just want to stop caring about the 'helpful' opinions others like to force on you about your life, then there are ways to shift your perspective and lead a much happier life in the process.

- Create For Self Your Own Life

In order to be more confident in your decisions and therefore be strong enough to dismiss what others say, creating a roadmap of where you want to go and how you're going to get there will bring more stability and less insecurity. By doing this, you will care much less about what other people are doing in comparison or what they think about you.

Create a list of goals, note where you are now in relation to them (with no negative judgment), and write out an action plan for how you can achieve them. You can make a one-week plan or a one-year plan – whatever you feel comfortable with on any subject – and you'll start to feel a sense of moving forward.

- Do Some 'All-Round' Self-Improvement

Self-improvement is a wonderful way to focus on ourselves, but often we tend to self-improve when the chips are down in certain areas of our lives. For example, if we want to improve our health, we may start to eat better and exercise more.

However, it can lead us to ignore other areas such as work, learning, or relationships. Focusing on more than one area will create a feeling that we're establishing abundance overall, which, in turn, will stop us from feeling lack and causing us to compare one area of our life to someone else's.

Write out a list of how you can improve each area of your life – perhaps learning something new for a dream job, an exercise routine to get healthy, or improving your social skills in order to make new friends. Do a little bit at a time for each area, and you'll soon grow more and more confident in yourself and where your life is heading.

**Remember That Everything Takes Time**

We're often made to think that certain life goals must happen by a certain time, but it doesn't always work out that way (this is when the comparison game can be at its strongest!) Try not to focus on specific time-frames and understand that you're always on your path to where you want to go.

People go along their own path at different speeds, and that's okay. Make peace with where you are, find all you can to appreciate your life no matter how small your successes, and believe that you will achieve your goals and dreams in your own timing – timing that's best for you and no one else.

## How to Stop Comparing Yourself to Others and Live Life to the Fullest

It's not a secret that social media is a major cause of depression nowadays. According to "Journal of Depression and Anxiety," people using social media are almost three times more likely to develop depression than people who use it less often. While comparing ourselves to others is in our nature, it's important to know how to stop comparing ourselves to others in a negative way.

1. Understand that you are shown the result, not the journey

The truth is that most people show only the highlights of their lives on social media. Usually, you don't get to see their everyday work and everything they have to do to maintain that quality of life. Also, you never know what they had to sacrifice for that success. Maybe for them, it doesn't seem to be a sacrifice, but for you, it would be one.

For example, you love spending time with your kids, and spending less time with them would be a sacrifice, while someone doesn't want to have kids at all, so they have a lot of time to pursue their goals and achieve success. Would it work for you? Probably not. So, always keep in mind that you see only the result, not the journey.

## 2. Become fulfilled

The best way to stop comparing yourself to others is to become fulfilled. Become a person who doesn't need to compare themselves to others. However, this is neither a short nor an easy journey. You should have enough passion and, what's more important, dedication and persistence.

## 3. Set goals, make an action plan

In case you haven't started your journey to success yet: set goals first. Be focused, don't set too many goals. Prioritize your goals and put all of your energy into pursuing one goal at a time.

After setting a goal, make an action plan. Keep in mind that both the plan and you should be flexible. If something doesn't go as planned, review all options you have at hand and choose the best one possible. Sometimes the Universe shows you ways you could have never imagined or thought of before. Sometimes the worst situation ever turns out to be a turning point leading you to success much faster.

Don't overestimate your power. As a human being, you have little control over other people and situations. Just make sure you choose the best possible option thrown at you.

## 4. Put your business first & social media aside

If you're only beginning your journey to success, comparing yourself to people who are in the middle of the journey or have already achieved great success is just wrong. You will never get to your destination if someone else's success distracts you from doing your job and discourages you. Spend as little time as possible on social media platforms and take care of your own business. Put your business first, always keeping in mind your end goal to motivate you.

## 5. You're going through life at your own pace

Everyone has their own path and pace. If you have already started moving towards your goal, and you know that you won't give up no matter what, sooner or later, you will achieve it anyway. The only difference between you and the people who already have what you desire is the amount of time spent working on a particular goal. Keep growing, keep improving yourself, and you will finally succeed.

Don't give up on a goal even if it takes you longer than you expected because you can always alter your plan. Stay flexible, and greet whatever the Universe gives you with gratitude.

Even if an obstacle comes into your path, make sure you consider it a blessing in disguise. Obstacles are opportunities to look at something from a different angle and learn something new. After all, there is no certain way to achieve success, so stay flexible, adjust, and you'll get there anyway.

## 6. Get rid of limiting beliefs

Get rid of your limiting beliefs ASAP. Don't get discouraged by the limiting beliefs that tell you "you are not worth it" or "it's impossible." Whenever you hear something like that from your relatives, friends, or your own mind, question those beliefs. Are they true, or are they deceiving you? Your mind may be deceiving you because it is against doing something extra and leaving its comfort zone. Fight your limiting beliefs!

## 7. Stop caring about other people's opinions

Stop caring about what people may think about you. Do your thing, be persistent, and stay focused. People don't think about you often anyway. It's better to try and fail than to regret that you've never even tried.

## 8. Treat yourself well

Be your own best friend and don't be too strict with yourself. Give yourself enough time to relax. Practice digital detoxing often or delete your social media accounts. You don't have to prove anything to anyone or impress other people. You also don't have to show them your progress. You don't have to tell them what's been happening in your life.

Focus on your own life and your happiness. Praise yourself and thank yourself for the work you've done. Be grateful for what you have achieved, and be proud of yourself. Don't give up even if you fail.

## Eight Amazing Things that Happen Once You Stop Comparing Yourself to Others

### 1. You will gain self-worth

When you compare your life to someone else's, it's usually the result of you not feeling good about yourself.

"Unfortunately, this game has few winners and leads you to the no-win trap of degrading or judging yourself or someone else. It can also lead to jealousy, anger, resentment, and even hatred for yourself or another person.

Once you let go of comparing your life to others, you allow yourself to focus on yourself and your own strengths, talents, and accomplishments. "If you're always looking at keeping up with other people or comparing yourself to other people, you're likely overlooking your own strengths and talents. You may even hide your talents and strengths,

## 2. You will clear your head

"You are essentially focused on this other person in an unhealthy manner, and wasting your precious energy on them instead of you." If you really want to have what someone else does, consider the notion that they probably worked diligently and gruelingly for what they have, and then turn that around and make it work for you by giving yourself the attention you crave and deserve

## 3. You embrace your individuality

When you compare your life to someone else's, you are setting up an unfair playing field from the start. Because no two people are exactly alike with exactly the same life experiences, Pfeffer says, it is virtually impossible to make a fair comparison between your life and someone else's. Embrace the uniqueness of what makes you who you are.

## 4. You gain self-acceptance

When you let go of caring about others' lives and their accomplishments and comparing yourself to them, you give yourself an enormous gift: the freedom to be you.

"This leads to increased self-acceptance which then boosts your self-esteem, confidence, and self-worth because you allow yourself to succeed at what you are good at,

### 5.You gain trust

When you stop comparing yourself to others, you are also increasing your trust in yourself and the universe; you gain faith that your skills and talents will be in demand and that you will come out on top. You will continue to have a brighter outlook and gain empowerment, and can focus on what you can control:

### 6. You have more gratitude

Letting go of comparisons facilitates what you should be grateful for in your own life. Write down your thoughts to stay on a healthy path. "Keeping a gratitude journal allows us to go back and reread all of the amazing things that happened in our lives and keeps us focused on the positive because we can see in black and white all of our wins.

### 7. You release a material focus

When you accept and feel grateful in your own life, you gain contentment, which transcends what you can buy.

"You embrace that you can be happy without the biggest house, the newest tech, the sleekest car – and you embrace your happiness depends solely on you. You embrace no external possession can make you happy,

### 8. You have a fulfilling life beyond social media

When you are in a good mental place, you put limits on your social media time and become better in the real world. "Realize social media and all  of the instant updates and notifications often drain our time, and our inner mean girl/guy thrives on the feeling of not being good enough

## Stop Comparing Yourself to Others to Improve Self-Esteem

Why should you stop comparing yourself to others? The main reason is that comparing yourself to others is destructive to your self-esteem. When you compare yourself to others, you might think they have it all together and believe you should be the same.

You might treat life as a competition and base your worth in comparison to what other people are good at, their looks, personalities, what they have, or what they've achieved. You may be too hard on yourself for not being like others and fail to see your own unique qualities. Comparing yourself to others is destructive to your self-esteem--and you can learn to stop it.

Basing your worth on other people is disempowering. What others do is outside of your control, and you can't change that. However, you can change the way you view yourself. Learn to stop comparing yourself to others and build your self-esteem.

### How to Stop Comparing Yourself to Others

- Realize that your worth comes from inside. It's who you are as a person regardless of externals. It does not depend on what others are doing.
- Know that looks can be deceiving. Everyone has their own issues and insecurities, even though they're often well hidden. Nobody has a perfect life. You may think someone is doing well, but you don't have the full picture.
- Stop worrying about what others are doing. You can't control what others are doing. It's disempowering and a waste of energy to worry about it. Instead, focus on

making your own life the best it can be.

- Forget about being right or wrong. Everyone has their own unique circumstances and strengths. What's right for one person may not be for another. Do what's right for you at the right time for you.
- Remember that there will always be someone better than you at something. That's life, no matter who you are. However, there are things you're better at, too. Realize that nobody's good at everything. Give yourself permission to try things out and to make mistakes.
- Have realistic expectations of yourself. Let go of perfectionism and be reasonable with your expectations.
- Know your own strengths and interests. Figure out what you're good at and what you like to do. If you're unsure, take the time to figure it out.
- Nurture your strengths. Do the things you're good at and enjoy.
- Focus on the positives about yourself. There are many positives about yourself, and it's a matter of seeing them. Focus on your good points. It might help to write them down or to practice gratitude.
- Embrace your individuality. Your uniqueness is what makes you special, and it's well worth embracing. You have so much value just by being yourself. Think of all the people who made a difference in this world just by being themselves.
- Know that life's not a competition. When you stop competing with others, it's liberating, and it gives you the freedom to be the best person you can be. Instead of competing with others, aim for personal growth.
- Find a purpose or meaning in what you do. What you're doing matters, and it's important to realize that.
- Enjoy the journey. Don't be overly concerned about outcomes or achievements. Instead, give yourself permission to enjoy the present moment, learn and grow.

Your life is your own unique journey, and it doesn't matter what others are doing. Be the best person you can be and embrace your individuality. Stop comparing yourself to others and give yourself permission to be yourself to improve your self-esteem.

# HOW TO BUILD SELF LOVE AND CONFIDENCE WITH A MORNING ROUTINE

- Choose to put yourself first.

Start by making a conscious choice to put yourself first. Use this affirmation to create positive emotions and connections:

I deserve to put myself first. I am worthy of spending time on myself.

Then, determine how much time you can dedicate to your morning ritual based on your current morning routine. Do you have a long commute? Do you have to get the kids ready for school? Think about how you currently spend your time and how much time you're willing to set aside for yourself.

Many people (including many men) recommend spending an hour on personal development first thing in the morning, but that's just not realistic for most women. Women take on the majority of household and childcare activities, so taking an hour for yourself may feel like a burden rather than an act of self-care.

Instead, you get to be in control of how you spend your time. Reverse engineer your morning ritual by choosing how much time you'd like to spend on yourself. There are no rules, no standards, and no have-to here. This is your time, and you need to feel comfortable with it.

You may choose to wake up 30 minutes or an hour earlier than normal to give yourself the time and space to really dedicate your practice. Or, you may decide that 10 minutes is all you can do in the morning. The time spent is not important; what is important is creating a realistic schedule you can stick to.

- Plan what you will do

Next, decide what you will do with the time you set aside. You may have time for one activity, or you may have enough time for two or three. There's no correct order of activities, and there's no perfect routine. It's about doing what feels good to you and making a commitment to yourself and your own personal or spiritual growth.

Here are a few examples of activities to include in your morning ritual:

**Meditation:** You can use a guided meditation app like Calm or Headspace, download my free guided meditations here, or simply pay attention to your breath. Meditation helps to calm anxiety, improve self-awareness, reduce stress, and improve your overall wellbeing.

- Find a comfortable and upright place to sit. Take a few deep breaths and watch the flow of your breath as it enters and leaves.
- Bring your focus to your heart, and as you breathe in, feel as if your heart is opening and softening; as you

breathe out, release any tension or resistance.

- Now bring into your heart either an image of yourself or repeat your name and hold yourself in your heart, tenderly and gently. Silently repeat, "May I be freed from self-doubt, may I be happy, may all things go well for me."
- Keep breathing into your heart, holding yourself with love, and repeating the words. This will generate a deep loving-kindness and appreciation for yourself.
- When you are ready, take a deep breath and let it go. Then go about your day with a caring heart and a smile on your lips.

**Journaling:** You can free write in a blank journal, choose a guided journal, find journal prompts online, or write about how you want to feel that day. Journaling can help you work through difficult emotions, identify your goals, or improve your creativity.

**Affirmations:** Affirmations help rewire your brain by replacing negative thoughts with positive ones. By proactively choosing your thoughts, you can shift your emotions and create positive behaviors to get the results you want. Check out this blog for 30 Affirmations for Confidence.

Here are 30 daily affirmations you can use to make building confidence a habit:

- I am aware of my gift to the world and share it freely.

- I am compassionate with others and myself.

- I am a positive being, aware of my potential.

- There are no blocks I cannot overcome.

- I love to meet other people and make new friends.

- I am my best source of motivation.

- Challenges are opportunities to grow and improve.

- I attract positive people into my life.

- I make a difference by showing up every day and doing my best.

- I am becoming a better version of myself one day at a time.

- I am worthy of having what I want.

- I am grateful for my journey and its lessons.

- I accept compliments easily.

- Everything is possible.

- I am creative and open to new solutions.

- I choose to embrace the mystery of life.

- I already have what I need.

- What I want is already here or on its way.

- I appreciate all that I have.

- I allow everything to be as it is.

- I enjoy going with the flow.

- The more I let go, the better I feel.

- I live from a place of abundance.

- I release anything that doesn't serve me.

- I believe in my abilities and express my true self with ease.

- All I need is within me.

- I am stronger than I seem.

- I am braver than I think.

- I have unshakable faith.

- Miracles are taking place in my life.

Practice saying these affirmations (or write them down) daily for 30 days. When you catch yourself in a negative thought process, consciously choose to say your affirmation out loud or use your journal to document your thoughts.

**Reading:** Whether it's novels, self-help, autobiographies, or historical fiction, reading helps you improve your vocabulary, critical thinking skills, focus, and concentration. Getting lost in your favorite book can also reduce stress!

**Exercise**: There are so many benefits to regular exercise, whether you choose to incorporate simple stretches, a short yoga practice, or a long run. Remember to be kind to your body, especially first thing in the morning. It's important to stay hydrated and not push yourself past what you can comfortably do.

**Creativity:** An often-overlooked ritual practice is doing something creative! Whether you choose to grab a coloring book, your knitting bag, a puzzle, or painting supplies, spending time being creative allows you to express yourself and connect with who you are. It also reduces stress, improves critical thinking, and gives you a sense of inner accomplishment.

**Prepare your ritual space.**

Next, determine a place where you will do your morning ritual and what you might need to do it.

- This depends on what you decided to incorporate into your morning ritual. If you want to include exercise, make sure you have enough space to move around and that the equipment you need is readily available. If you want to meditate for five or 10 minutes, you can choose to sit on the side of your bed or supported on the floor.

- If you can, choose a space where you won't be interrupted and space you can return to each day. Make this your sacred space. If you live with family or roommates, let them know about your space and the time you plan to do your morning ritual.

- Place everything you need for your morning ritual in this space; grab your journal and a pen, the book you want to read, a meditation pillow or yoga mat, or your art supplies.

- You may choose to make your space more inviting by including a cozy sweater or blanket, lighting a candle, dimming the lights, or bringing in a warm cup of coffee or tea.

## Commit to a daily ritual

- It's time to commit to your new morning ritual! This is your time and your space to fill with things that light you up. To help the habit stick, try to commit to waking up at the same time every morning to start your routine.

- If you have trouble waking up at the same time, try to set an intention before you go to bed. The night before you start your morning ritual, set the alarm, then silently set an intention to commit to your practice. You can try something like:

- I will wake up feeling refreshed and excited to start my new morning ritual.

- When you wake up the next morning, you'll feel more energized and ready to set aside the time for yourself. It might be hard at first, but keep going. Experiment with what feels right for you.

- Maybe that's making a cup of coffee or tea before beginning your morning routine, or maybe sitting quietly with your warm beverage is your perfect morning routine! You can do your morning ritual immediately after you wake up, or you can choose to take a shower or brush your teeth first.

- This is your time and your practice, so the only thing that matters is that you're taking the time for yourself that fits into your lifestyle. That way, it becomes easier to make it a daily habit.

## The Takeaway

A morning ritual helps you build self-worth from the inside, from a strong sense of inner wisdom that you are enough just the way you are. You don't need validation from other people, and you can give even more to others by putting yourself first.

Setting aside a few minutes each morning to do the things that light you up sends a signal to your brain that you deserve to put yourself first. The more time you spend with yourself, the more you'll start to believe that you ARE worthy and you do deserve to take the time to do the things you love.

Take action now: Build a habit around your morning ritual. Decide the one, two, or three things you want to incorporate into your morning, and commit to doing those things for 30 days.

Taking this time for YOU is so important for your wellbeing and sense of self-worth. We don't often give ourselves permission to just be with ourselves, so by creating your own sacred time each morning, you're telling the Universe that you're committed to putting yourself first.

# STEPS TO SELF LOVE
# AND CONFIDENCE